How to Die Without a Lawyer

Also by Mary Clement

Freedom to Die:
People, Politics, and the Right-to-Die Movement

How to Die Without a Lawyer

A PRACTICAL GUIDE TO CREATING AN ESTATE PLAN WITHOUT PAYING LEGAL FEES

Mary Clement

St. Martin's Griffin, New York

Designed by Kate Nichols

ISBN 0-312-24401-0

First Edition: January 2000

10 9 8 7 6 5 4 3 2 1

To my son, Jamie,

who has been steadfast in his support

throughout the journey

I have done my best to give you accurate information in this book. However, laws are constantly changing and are open to various interpretations, often within the same state. This is the beauty and the peril of the law. If you use this book, it is your responsibility to verify that the facts and the law contained herein are applicable to your situation. The facts of each individual case are different and may change the application of the law. If you want the security of legal advice guaranteed by warranty, please see a lawyer.

Contents

How to Die Without a Lawyer

Introduction

If a man dies and leaves his estate in an uncertain condition, the lawyers become his heirs.

—Edgar Watson Howe

WHY YOU NEED THIS BOOK

Lawyers love estates. Especially big estates. And most especially big *probate* estates. Probate is the procedure that each state requires to settle legally the estate of a deceased person and to transfer his "probate property"—that is, property that stands in the deceased's name alone at the time of death or that will require action on the part of the executor to transfer. *All property passing under a will is "probate property."* The bigger the probate estate, the bigger the legal fee. It only makes sense, therefore, to avoid probate and thereby to avoid lawyers. And that is exactly what this book will help you do. You will act as your own lawyer, so that neither you nor your beneficiaries will incur the exorbitant expenses that lawyers charge. You will die with nary a lawyer in sight.

Even worse than wasting money on lawyers is what happens if you *don't* execute a will or use some other valid method to transfer your property after you die. Your property will be distributed to your spouse and children under the "intestate succession" law of your state. Thus the legal system steps in to ensure that the proper assets are distributed to the intended beneficiaries, to interpret potentially harmful language errors, to interpret ambiguities, to guess how you feel about futile medical treatment, to appoint a stranger to manage your finances, and to comfort your children when the judge assigns a stranger to raise your children and handle their property. If you have neither spouse nor child and no relatives qualify under law to inherit your property, it will go to the government—not a happy resting place for the rewards and remains of a lifetime of work and sacrifice. Without any planning, you are inviting a swarm of expensive professionals to devour the many thousands of dollars that would otherwise go to your loved ones.

The curious thing is that for all our loathing of lawyers, we fail to take the very steps that will help us avoid them—and fairly easy steps they are. Think about it. Approximately 75% of Americans die without even a will, to say nothing about other estate planning devices. Roughly 85% fail to execute a living will or health care proxy, too many ignoring the reality that they may spend countless years and thousands or hundreds of thousands of dollars hooked up to life-support systems they vow they would never want.

When we do take action, we fall for the planning that will benefit our lawyer upon our death. In thirty years of signing wills and their codicils, no lawyer ever mentioned the serious drawbacks of probate to me. The words "living trust" never crossed a pair of smiling lips. Avoiding probate is not in their financial best interest, since probate is such a cash cow for attorneys.

Many people consider estate planning a matter of executing a will. In reality, a will is an important but *small portion* of a well-executed estate plan, and merely executing a will ignores the enormous benefits of nonprobate property. Passing your estate through your will is the most expensive, vulnerable, and time-consuming way to pass property at death. In reading this book, you will learn how to write your own will, avoid probate, and create a living trust, as well as the advantages and disadvantages of other probate-saving devices.

You will be advised to take a simple precaution that too many lawyers either accidentally or intentionally overlook: the inclusion of the "no-contest clause." The absence of this clause can subject the estate to unnecessary litigation by opening the door to unsatisfied beneficiaries. Legal disputes over a will can be as financially and emotionally demanding as any dispute you might have the misfortune to experience.

The legal establishment has succeeded in mystifying the process of writing even the simplest of wills. People avoid writing their own will for fear of their imagined inadequacies. On the other hand, going to an attorney, they correctly suspect, will cost them a considerable fee. The result is either inaction or the lawyers becoming the beneficiaries. *How to Die Without a Lawyer* demystifies the process, and, for a small fraction of the cost of hiring a lawyer, it will provide the reader's beneficiaries with an estate easy to settle without an attorney.

The easiest estates to settle are the ones that are well planned during the lifetime of the deceased. Comprehensive estate planning includes deciding who will inherit your property, deciding who will take care of your young children and their inheritance if you die while they are still minors, putting procedures and devices in place to minimize probate costs at your death, attempting to reduce federal and state estate taxes, and arranging for someone to make medical and financial decisions on your behalf in the event that you become incompetent and unable to make these decisions for yourself. How to Die Without a Lawyer *reveals the secrets of trusts and estates law, enabling you, the reader, to produce the same work as the professionals, without the legal fees and with the added benefit of your estate being more financially advantageous to your beneficiaries than to your lawyer.*

At no time in history, however, is there more need for "affairs to be in order" than now. The Dow Jones has become part of popular culture, and half of American households now have exposure to the stock market, either directly, through mutual funds, or through the ubiquitous 401(k) retirement plans. The record-setting advances of the stock market in recent years have increased the involvement of many Americans in the market and bestowed material bounty as never before. The run-up in the stock market since 1994 has added an extra $10 trillion to the assets of American households.

Just as striking are the technological advances that have changed the face of stock trading as well as the face of death. A decade ago, anyone who wanted to buy or sell a stock had to call his broker to get the price, and then pay a hefty sum to complete the trade. Today, stock prices are available to anyone with a television, radio, or computer, and investors can trade on-line for as little as $10 a transaction. The striking result of these changes is that more people have more assets. More assets and more responsibilities. More need for estate planning.

Advances in technology have also given rise to the fear of dying in the cold, dehumanizing clutches of modern medical technology, and this has given a major boost to public acceptance of a hastened death. Americans are justifiably uneasy about the cost and the impersonal technological arrogance of modern medical care. They fear a prolonged death that diminishes their dignity and burdens their loved ones, while bringing individual lawyers and the entire legal system to the bedside. Hence, the need has arisen for advance directives—living wills, health care proxies, and nonhospital do-not-resuscitate orders—to protect the ill and infirm from a prolonged, agonizing, and expensive dying experience. This book ensures that the reader's last wishes will be honored, sparing family members costly and protracted legal battles.

How to Die Without a Lawyer includes all the major aspects of estate planning, including the assurance that your last wishes will be followed if you become incapable of making your own medical decisions. The book explains what choices you have, how these choices work, and the advantages and disadvantages of the different options.

Each chapter covers a major estate planning concern. The beginning of each chapter gives you an overview of the material covered in that chapter, so you can select only those subjects that concern you. The role of the particular subject in the overall scope of estate planning is explained. I encourage you to use this book in any way that is advantageous to you, including underlining, highlighting, and making notes in the margin. A glossary at the back of the book will help you with unfamiliar words and phrases.

Sample estate planning documents—such as wills, affidavits, codicils, financial powers of attorney, living wills, health care proxies, nonhospital do-not-resuscitate orders, and living trusts—are available in the appendix at the back of the book. These sample documents and suggested personal clauses will familiarize you with what language to use in your own documents.

How to Die Without a Lawyer is free of legal jargon (even though it is written by a lawyer), interesting to read, and easy to follow. Lists are used, important concepts are highlighted, and the subject matter is concise. My intent is to make things as easy and painless as possible. You will congratulate yourself on your foresight and organization, knowing that your survivors will appreciate you even more for your considerate planning.

WHO NEEDS THIS BOOK

How to Die Without a Lawyer is designed for residents of all states *except Louisiana*, which has a legal system different from all the other states, based on the Napoleonic Code.

You need this book even if you have every intention of seeing a lawyer. You need to be an informed consumer. You need to know what options are available to you and what questions to ask. You need to be aware of what lawyers usually withhold from clients. They don't lie; they just omit. If you go into their offices knowledgeable, you will get better results and you won't waste time and money.

The book is useful for people with estates of any amount who prefer to avoid lawyers but realize that life entails certain "legalities" that must be periodically addressed. Methods of avoiding probate work equally well for estates worth thousands of dollars as for those worth millions. And *all* responsible parents need to address two major questions: Who will raise my children if I die? and How can I best provide financial support for my children if I die? If you don't answer these questions, the judge will answer them for you. You will also want a *durable power of attorney for financial matters,* giving a trusted person the authority to handle your finances if you become incapacitated. Either you do it now while you are competent, or the court will name a stranger when you're not.

For people with estates exceeding the federal estate tax exemption (see chapter 13 for more on the personal estate tax exemption), I advise you to consult an attorney. This tax exemption is for individual estates that are worth less than $675,000 in 2000, increasing to $1,000,000 in 2006 and beyond. For couples, the amount also increases until 2006 when it peaks at $2,000,000. This book does not attempt to deal with taxes at all, except in the most minimal way. Tax laws are continually being revised and amended. As a consequence, tax planning has to be constantly reviewed and updated. The issue of taxes is best left to tax specialists—either tax lawyers or accountants.

Whether you are single or a member of a couple, this book enables you to make legally binding provisions for beneficiaries who inherit your property. By following the instructions on signing and witnessing, you will conform to the necessary formalities of a will. You can set up your own living trust, allowing you to transfer property after your death without attorney's fees or court involvement. You will avoid probate, so near and dear to the hearts of lawyers.

The book is for those of you who know that, with my help, you can do just as good a job as a lawyer—for less money and irritation. Careful planning will produce smooth results. Addressing these issues before they occur removes the trauma of court-appointed guardians and proxies who know nothing about your personal, medical, or financial wishes and leave your family feeling powerless, penniless, and distraught.

WHEN YOU NEED A LAWYER

No state law requires that a will or a probate-avoiding device be prepared or approved by a lawyer. In most cases, a will drafted by a lawyer is not as custom-tailored as you might assume. Quite likely, the lawyer has created a standardized form on a computer into which he types your name, the names of the people to whom your property will go, the guardian of any minor children, the name of the executor, and any other pertinent information. The attorney then prints out the form for you to sign, asks you for $500, $600, $700 for his labors, bids you farewell, and shakes your hand good-bye.

However, you may want and need a lawyer, depending on your situation, which may be very simple and easily handled with a couple of documents. Many people will decide that with the aid of this book, they can do their estate planning without a lawyer. Or, you may need a lawyer's help for tax planning or for the creation of complex devices to control your property long after your death. You may fall somewhere in the middle. Whatever you decide, *How to Die Without a Lawyer* will provide you with the legal issues and tools to make the best choices and to keep your legal bills to a minimum.

There are some situations for which even the most clear-thinking, knowledgeable person needs professional help with will writing and estate planning. Here are some common circumstances for which a lawyer's services are recommended:

➡ You want a special needs trust to protect the assets of a disabled child or family member who will require long-term care.
➡ You own part of a small business and have concerns about the rights of surviving owners as well as your own ownership share.
➡ You want to establish a trust other than a simple family pot trust or child's trust. You may want everything put in trust so that your children receive only the income for their lifetime, with final distribution outright to your grandchildren.

➡ You want to leave property in a more complex manner than this book describes. For example, you may want to leave property to be used by your surviving spouse during his lifetime, and then to go to your children after the spouse's death.

➡ Your individual estate exceeds the federal estate tax threshold. You will be subject to substantial federal estate taxation unless you engage in federal estate tax planning.

➡ You are in a second or subsequent marriage where at least one of you has children from a prior marriage. You are concerned about possible conflicts between your spouse and your children over your property distributions.

If you decide at any point during the process that you need the advice of an attorney, the knowledge gained here will put you ahead of the game. You already know the basics and have given thought to what you want, so you can confidently spend less time with the lawyer. Moreover, you will have learned how and why to avoid probate, and you can therefore enrich your beneficiaries instead of your lawyer by transferring your assets into probate-saving devices. I guarantee, your beneficiaries will thank you even though your lawyer won't.

WHERE TO OBTAIN THE NECESSARY DOCUMENTS

Estate planning requires that you complete a number of documents. Sample estate planning documents, such as wills, living wills, and living trusts, are available in the appendix. If, for whatever reason, you choose not to use them, I recommend the following sources, where documents can be purchased at a reasonable cost:

1. All of the documents discussed in this book can be purchased in most stationery stores. If one store doesn't have the forms, try another store. They are *not* hard to find. The disadvantage of these generic forms is that some of them can be quite skeletal, covering only the bare basics. But they are certainly better than nothing.

2. Comprehensive living wills, health care proxies and nonhospital do-not-resuscitate orders, for *New York State and Arizona*
   only, along with questions and answer booklets for each document, and an informational document for the survivors
   (which provides a place to write the information your survivors need at the time of your death and the location of all
   your vital information) can be obtained from:

   Mary Clement, Esq.
   Gentle Closure, Inc.
   60 Santa Susana Lane
   Sedona, AZ 86336
   tel: (520) 282-0170
   fax: (520) 282-0286
   e-mail: Marydclem@aol.com

3. State-specific living will and health care proxy forms for all
   fifty states are available from:

   Choice in Dying
   1035 30th Street NW
   Washington, DC 20007
   1-800-989-WILL
   e-mail: cid@choices.org

4. Nolo Press offers numerous legal self-help books with estate
   planning documents and some software. These may be obtained from:

   Nolo Press
   950 Parker Street
   Berkeley, CA 94710
   tel: 1-800-992-6656
   e-mail: NOLOSUB@NOLOPRESS.COM

Now that you have glimpsed the importance of getting your affairs in
order—regardless of the amount of your estate—and the ease of ac-
complishing this task with the help of this book, you are ready to learn
some of the specifics of estate planning. I will begin by examining top-

ics that lay the groundwork for preparing your own will. The actual creating of your will follows. We will do this together, step by step. Estate planning is nothing to be afraid of. It is simply the strategy and the documents you utilize to accomplish what you want. That's it. My job is to help you with information and support. You're in charge now!

PART I

Laying the Groundwork for Creating a Will

1

An Overview
of Estate Planning

*To my dear friend Mrs. George Hale, I give and bequeath the
satisfaction of being remembered in my Will; and
I leave my lawyer, Huber Lewis, the task of explaining to my
relatives why they didn't get a million dollars apiece.*

—from the will of Edwin O. Swain,
who died penniless

Your estate includes all the property you own when you die. Estate
planning is the development of a plan to provide for effective and
orderly distribution of an individual's assets at the time of death. Good
estate planning is more than drafting wills and contemplating tax consequences. Everyone wants to minimize his or her tax liabilities, but an
overemphasis on taxes can substantially alter the ownership and enjoyment of your and your beneficiaries' assets.

A glance at this book's table of contents reveals the breadth of estate planning. While each area carries its own set of rules and considerations, no one part can be viewed in a vacuum. Hence, property
transferred by will cannot be considered without reviewing those assets
that can legally pass *outside* of a will, such as jointly owned property
and retirement assets. Also, the well-being of minor children must be
considered in tandem with wills, trusts, naming a guardian of the child
(responsible for the supervision and control of a minor child), naming
a guardian of the property (for safekeeping and financial management
of the child's assets), naming children as beneficiaries of life insurance
and other probate-avoiding techniques, disinheritance, and a comparison of the four major ways of leaving property to a minor, including the
Uniform Transfers to Minors Act.

The process of developing an estate plan begins with assembling copies of deeds, stockholders' agreements, separation agreements, insurance policies, and the like. A complete profile of your assets will allow you to determine what you own and subsequently what you can give away. You can also determine whether the estate will have a liquidity problem; that is, will there be enough cash or other liquid assets to pay taxes, administration expenses, and funeral expenses?

How the assets are owned is equally important as *what* you own. An individual will often speak of "his" property when, in fact, the asset is held by *both* partners of the marriage as tenants by the entirety. This property cannot pass under "his" will, but, instead, will immediately pass to the surviving spouse at his death. Liquid assets to satisfy cash requirements would not, therefore, be available from this property. Additional assets may be restrained from liquidation by the terms of a shareholder's partnership, or pension agreement. There is the added possibility that assets may be held as "community property," which is a form of joint marital property ownership, popular in eight Western states. Very generally, and with some exceptions, all property acquired after marriage and before permanent separation is considered to belong equally to both spouses in community property states. All of these jointly owned assets affect the size of the gross estate, the amount of allowable deductions, and the distribution of the assets.

In selecting the format for passing assets to your beneficiaries, you basically have two vehicles: a trust and a will. A revocable living trust can accomplish most people's main estate planning goals: leaving property to loved ones while avoiding probate and, if possible, saving on estate taxes as well. It eliminates the need and expense of probate as well as the entanglement of the court for the transfer of your property.

However, a living trust is not by itself a complete estate plan. You still need a will. A will specifies who gets the property mentioned in the document when you die. It also provides a place to name your executor (the person who carries out the terms of the will); to insert a no-contest clause (which automatically disinherits anyone who unsuccessfully challenges your will); to include a simultaneous death clause (which provides that if the testator—you, the creator of the will—and a beneficiary die under circumstances in which it is impossible to determine the order of death, then you are considered to have survived the beneficiary, unless your will provides otherwise); to forgive debts; and to name a trusted friend or relative to raise any minor children and to manage their property until they reach the majority age as determined by their state—usually age 18.

There are other means by which estates may be distributed. Arrangements may deal only with specialized assets, such as title to property held as joint tenants with a right of survivorship, and beneficiary designations for bank accounts, stocks and bonds, life insurance proceeds, employee death benefits, individual retirement accounts (IRAs), and deferred compensation plans. Comprehensive estate planning may also include the use of irrevocable trusts used to exert control over the beneficiary's right to the trust property. The income from such trusts might be used to pay for education, protect an unreliable beneficiary from squandering trust principal, or provide security for those with special physical or mental disabilities.

More than anything, you must be aware of the human element. Your estate plan won't be satisfactory to you or your beneficiaries unless you take human concerns into account. You must draw on your own life experiences and use your intuitive judgment in making decisions about your estate. Many people face no serious personal problems in their planning. They are clear about who the beneficiaries will be and foresee no personal or legal conflict over their estate after they are gone. Other people must deal with more difficult human dynamics, like the painful decision to disinherit a child. Money and possessions are not known for bringing out the best in people, and you may envision problematic scenarios as you consider the distribution of your estate.

A central goal of estate planning is to avoid conflict to the greatest degree reasonably possible. A good estate plan is an accurate reflection of your common sense and honesty regarding the strengths, weaknesses, and genuine needs of family members and possibly friends. Before you begin your plan, assess your circumstances and decide how you might be able to resolve foreseeable conflicts.

POTENTIAL CONFLICTS AND SOLUTIONS

#1. You may want to leave unequal amounts of your estate to your children, but you don't want to leave the impression that you are favoring one child over the other.

Solution: Write a detailed letter explaining how and why you reached your decision, while at the same time expressing your love and good wishes for all children involved. Attach this letter to your estate planning documents (will and living trust), where your children can read it after you are gone. You can always amend the documents if circumstances change over time. This letter is a personal one between you and your children, requiring neither witnessing nor notarizing.

#2. Sometimes parents find it necessary to disinherit a child, leaving him nothing by will or trust.

Solution: It is perfectly legal to disinherit a child, but not a spouse, who has a right to inherit a certain percentage of your estate as determined by state law. Parents often feel it too harsh to completely disinherit a child. To soften the blow, you can leave the child a nominal amount and include a no-contest clause in your will. This clause states that if the will is contested by a beneficiary, he will receive nothing under the will if the challenge is unsuccessful. Odds are he will take the certain amount rather than risk the cost of a lawsuit and the good possibility of losing the bequest by virtue of the no-contest clause. Once again, write a letter explaining your reasoning and know that you can change your will at a later date.

Deciding to disinherit or "almost" disinherit a child is painful for a parent. One resolution to the problem, if grandchildren exist, is to create an educational trust for each offspring of the disinherited child, leaving each a specified amount for college or other post–high school education.

#3. People often worry about the effect of leaving money or property to a beneficiary they feel is too young or immature to handle it. Chronological age is not always the determinant. The beneficiary, usually an offspring in this case, may be a drug abuser or may belong to a cult that too easily could become the direct recipient.

Solution: You could leave a moderate amount outright and then leave the rest in trust to be released upon the child reaching a certain age. A common age used for these situations is 35. Another alternative is to give the beneficiary *only* the income from a trust for his lifetime. The beneficiary's children or a charitable institution could be the recipient of the trust principal outright when the income beneficiary dies.

#4. Unmarried couples wonder where they stand with regard to inheriting each other's estate.

Solution: Unmarried (lesbian, gay, or heterosexual) couples have no legal right, unlike a spouse, to inherit each other's money or property. However, unmarried people have total discretion to leave their property to whomever they choose, as long as they are competent. Sometimes hostile family members who have long disapproved of a nontraditional relationship will demand proof of the competency of the testator. Added precautions can be part of good planning here. To preclude future legal action, it is the better part of wisdom to establish by clear evidence that the testator was competent and not under duress or undue influence when he executed the estate plan. This can be accomplished by videotaping the signing and notarizing the documents, even though neither is required by law.

#5. A major concern of parents with minor children is who will take care of the children if both parents die.

Solution: There are really two issues to look at here: Who will be the personal guardian, responsible for raising the children and dealing with their day-to-day activities? and Who will be the property guardian, supervising the handling of all assets until the state or the parents feel the children are old enough to handle the property themselves? These jobs can be done by one person if that person has the expertise to perform both functions. If not, two people can be appointed—one to raise the child and another to supervise the finances. Trust and respect are characteristics needed for both jobs, but a child's input may determine the compatibility of all involved when appointing the personal guardian.

Also, after you have decided on the individual(s) but before you commit them in writing, make sure you ask if they are willing to accept the tasks. Some people are unable to handle the added responsibilities and would perceive their new role as a hardship. Others are flattered and accept immediately. There is nothing positive for your children in either living with people who don't want them or having their finances managed by someone who resents doing it. As I said earlier, the object of successful estate planning is to avoid or at least minimize conflict.

#6. People often ask how much should be said to family members about the estate planning that has taken place.

Solution: Certainly you need to communicate with people to whom you are giving responsibility for your minor children and with those supervising the distribution of your property after you die. What about telling beneficiaries what they will inherit? Do you want to give your heirs copies of your will? Do you want to tell people what you have already done, or perhaps state that you are open to any reasonable suggestions? It depends largely on your style. The approach you use should be personal and individual; it will depend on the nature of your relationships and your general tendency to divulge or withhold personal information. However, there are benefits to talking with family members, or at the very least mentioning that estate planning is or has taken place.

Future conflicts can often be avoided by inviting conversation now. If children are old enough for reasoned judgment, it is wise to get their views on with whom they would like to live. Discuss who will be appointed executor. The executor is the one who will manage the estate and gather and distribute the assets as you have specified in your will or trust. It is also possible that a child might have deep attachment to a family heirloom or other items that mean nothing to his siblings. One of my children specifically requested the books that fill the bookcases in our living room. If you are comfortable with the idea, open the conversation with your beneficiaries about feelings and preferences. Disputes are often over things that do *not* involve money. *The goal of planning is satisfaction for all parties.* Openly discussing certain matters can go a long way toward avoiding conflicts in the future.

This chapter has helped you focus in a general way on what you own and on the different means by which your estate may be distributed. I hope it has also brought an awareness of the human element into estate planning. You are dealing with possessions and assets, but human beings, with their frailties and sensitivities, must drive the process of estate planning for it to be successful. Considering these human dynamics *now* will determine how you are remembered in the future. From here on, I will concentrate on specific topics and issues that you need to know.

Property Rules for Married Couples

To my wife, Jen Eberhart, one-third of my estate. It is my earnest desire and everlasting wish that the above named adulteress and fiend in human form, to whose wiles I fell victim while temporarily separated from my first wife, this harlot whose insidious lies, poured in to my ear daily, caused me to take the step which made a reconciliation with my first wife impossible, this she-devil who, in an effort to ruin my good name, has for the last three years circulated the most damnable lies about me ever uttered by human tongue, this unnamable beast, who has made life for me a living hell for the last three years or more, and by whom I stand in daily fear of being murdered while asleep I repeat, it is my everlasting wish that this woman, whom I am compelled by law to call my wife, shall not receive one cent more of my very modest estate than she is entitled to under the laws of the State of Pennsylvania.

—from the will of Peter Eberhart

Although people are generally free to leave their property as they wish, there are state property ownership laws that affect how *married people* can distribute their property. These laws determine what you own individually and, therefore, what is yours to leave to others. If you are married or in the process of getting a divorce, these laws will give your surviving spouse the right to claim a certain percentage of your estate. The epigraph above from Peter Eberhart's will shows how a surviving spouse cannot be disinherited, no matter how badly the deceased spouse would like to do just that!

If you give away property you don't own or fail to give your spouse the minimum amount as determined by state law, you are leaving a contentious and expensive lawsuit to your family.

You need to read this chapter if:

1. you are married or in the process of getting a divorce; and
2. you plan to leave the majority of your estate to someone other than your spouse; or
3. you do not have voluntary, written approval from the other spouse that you want to ignore the state's ownership rules.

You can skip this chapter if:

1. you are *single, divorced, or widowed;* or
2. you are married and intend to leave the overwhelming portion of your estate to your spouse.

If you fall into the category of one who needs this chapter, you will need to answer the following questions:

1. Are you "married" for estate planning purposes?
2. Do you live in a "community property" state or a "common law" state?
3. What property is yours to give away when you die?
4. What (if anything) are you required to leave to your surviving spouse?

ARE YOU "MARRIED" FOR ESTATE PLANNING PURPOSES?

Most people know if they are married; it's usually not a complicated question. However, in some situations and for will-writing purposes, a person's marital status is not always so clear. For example, if you are legally separated but not yet divorced, your about-to-be former spouse still has the right to inherit one-third or one-half of your estate. So, are you married?

Divorce Pending or Annulment

You remain *legally married* until a court issues a formal decree of divorce or annulment, signed by a judge in the United States. This is true even if you and your spouse have filed for divorce or annulment or have lived apart for an extended period.

If you are divorced or your marriage has been annulled, you are under no legal obligation to leave anything to your spouse. The effect of a divorce upon the validity of a will varies from state to state. In most states, if you have already executed your will leaving property to your spouse from whom you are now divorced, that gift is null and void. The spouse automatically disappears from the will. It is as if the spouse has already died.

If you are no longer married, you should write another will, keeping your estate plan as up-to-date as possible.

Tip: A beneficiary's name on a life insurance policy does not become void automatically after a divorce. The former spouse named as the beneficiary will usually remain as the beneficiary until such time as the policyholder makes a legal change during his lifetime.

Legal Separation

You are legally married for purposes of a will even if you are legally separated, plan to eventually divorce, or have lived apart for an extended time. *You are legally married until you get the divorce decree.*

If you think you are divorced but have never seen the final decree (or dissolution, as some states call it), contact the clerk of the court in the county where you think the divorce was granted. You must give the clerk your name, your former spouse's name, and the date of the divorce, or as close to the date as you know.

Common Law Marriages

In some states, an unmarried man and woman can automatically become legally married if they live together *and* "hold themselves out" as married (have common ownership of property *and* introduce the other person as a spouse). Common law marriages are recognized in Alabama, Colorado, Georgia, Idaho, Iowa, Kansas, Montana, New Hampshire, Ohio, Oklahoma, Pennsylvania, Rhode Island, South Carolina, Texas, Utah, and the District of Columbia.

Tip: *There is no such thing as a common law divorce.* A formal divorce proceeding with a formal decree of divorce, signed by a judge in the United States, is necessary to end a common law marriage. If you live in a community property state (Arizona, California, Idaho, Louisiana, Nevada, New Mexico, Texas, Washington, or Wisconsin), the court may divide the property "equitably" (fairly) if the standard division of property into one-half results in unfairness to one of the parties. In common law states (District of Columbia and all other states; common law states are not the same as states that recognize common law marriages), assets accumulated during marriage are theoretically divided "fairly" at the divorce. In practice, "fair" is left to the discretion of the judge. A thorough discussion of community property states and common law states is presented later in this chapter.

Remarriage to Former Spouse

With increasing frequency, divorced spouses are remarrying each other. In some states, such as New York, the remarriage "revives" the inheritance under an existing will that the divorce had determined to be null and void, unless another will has already been drawn up since the divorce.

Same-Sex Marriages

At the present time, *no state* legally recognizes a marriage between two people of the same sex, even when a religious ceremony has performed and sanctioned the alliance.

DO YOU LIVE IN A COMMUNITY PROPERTY STATE OR A COMMON LAW STATE?

If you and your spouse are leaving all of your property to each other, it makes no difference which kind of state you live in. If you are married and leaving significant property to others, read on.

Your Domicile

You need to know which state is your domicile. "Domicile" is the legal term for where you permanently live. You can only have one domicile, although you may have many residences or homes. *The state of your domicile governs your marital property, except for real estate, which is governed by the law of the state or country in which it is located, re-gardless of your domicile.* If you have only *one home,* it's easy. Your domicile is the state in which that home is located. If you have *more than one home in different states,* you need to determine in which state you are domiciled.

Why Establishing Your Domicile Is Important

If you own property in more than one state, you face the possibility that all of the states will impose domicile on you. This action entails the states not only reaching out to claim death taxes and their probate allocation, but also reviewing your past income tax records. These issues are not raised during your lifetime, but they become a serious reality upon your death, often resulting in litigation and, of course, expense to the estate. Many a naive layperson's inaccurate notion of his legal residence has led to devastating results when precautionary steps so easily could have been taken. So, beat them to it! Establish your domicile during your lifetime, so no ambiguities exist when you die.

Your domicile will also provide the governing law with respect to many significant estate planning issues. For example, the law of the domicile

1. governs the rights of the surviving spouse and children;
2. determines the validity of the will by providing rules of construction to interpret the will; and
3. governs the administration of the estate.

How Your Domicile Is Determined

Your actions, not your words, determine your domicile. There is no single explanation that sets forth the criteria, but the courts have looked at various factors when determining domicile. They include:

➡ ownership of dwelling
➡ percentage of time spent in the state where the dwelling is located
➡ homestead tax exemption in states where it applies
➡ other real estate holdings
➡ occupation
➡ business interests and activities
➡ filing of tax returns

- voter registration and proof of actually having voted
- automobile registration
- driver's license
- location of bank accounts and safe-deposit boxes
- location of a will
- recital of domicile in a will
- ownership of cemetery lot
- statement of residence via affidavit
- church, synagogue, mosque, or other religious membership
- civic and club participation
- union membership

Generally speaking, steps should be taken to reduce contacts that point to unwanted domiciles and to strengthen contacts that point to the desired domicile. Spend a majority of time in the domiciliary residence, maintain records of time spent in each state, and obtain a new insurance agent and new insurance policies in the desired domicile.

A strong case for a domicile exists when the state of residence for the entire family and the state of employment are the same. Children sent to local schools and local doctors and dentists increase the credibility. Another persuasive tack is to consistently declare the desired domicile on all documents that require a statement of domicile or residence, such as passports, contracts, deeds, leases, travel documents, hotel registration, and credit applications. Common sense serves as the polestar in most decision making.

Which Kind of State Do You Live In?

There are two types of states for purposes of deciding what you own and what you must leave to your surviving spouse. The state that is your domicile is the state that governs your marital property. There are community property states and common law states. The community property states are Arizona, California, Idaho, Nevada, New Mexico, Texas, Washington, and Wisconsin (and Louisiana, which I do not address in this book). Common law states are all of the remaining states and the District of Columbia.

What Property Is Yours to Give away When You Die?

Now that you know your domicile and thus the kind of state you live in, you must look at whether you actually own, and therefore are entitled to give away, this property in your estate. If you live in one of the eight community property states, then you only need to read "Community Property States" below. If you live in one of the common law states, you only need to read "Common Law States" below.

Community Property States

The concept of community property comes to us from Spanish settlers and explorers who established residence in some of our Western states. More recently it was adopted in Wisconsin, where it is called "marital property." *The community property rule is this: All property earned or acquired by either spouse during marriage is owned in equal one-half shares by each spouse—except for "separate property" as defined below.*

In community property states, all property that isn't community property is owned entirely by one spouse and is called "separate property." *Property owned by one spouse prior to the marriage and property given as separate property to one spouse as a gift or through inheritance is separate property.*

Once again, it is important to note that the ownership of real estate is controlled by the law of the state or country in which the property is located, not the state in which you are domiciled. For example, you and your spouse live, work, pay taxes, and vote in New York (a common law state) and you own a vacation house in Arizona (a community property state). Your house in Arizona will be transferred under the community property laws of Arizona at the time of your death, while your New York home will transfer under the common law rules of that state.

Community Property in Community Property States

In community property states, community property is owned in equal shares by a husband and wife. Each spouse, that is, owns 50% of this property. Community property consists of the following:

➡ all employment income received by either spouse during marriage—even if it is kept in separate accounts

➡ all property bought with employment income received by either spouse during the marriage

➡ all gifts made to both spouses

➡ all wedding gifts

➡ all inheritances made to both spouses

➡ all income earned from previously owned property (Only true in Texas and Idaho. Wisconsin's statute is unclear, so see an attorney if this state's law affects you. In all other states it is separate property.)

➡ the proportion of military and private employment pensions attributed to earnings during the marriage

➡ all property that comes to the marriage as separate property but that was deliberately transferred into community property by one of the spouses during the marriage; for example, one spouse could transfer the title of a separately owned house into both spouses' names

➡ all property that started out as separate property but has become so mixed ("commingled" in legalese) with community property that it is indistinguishable from the community property

Suppose that Ellie and Bill live in Washington, a community property state. Ellie inherits one hundred shares of AT&T stock (separate property). She puts these stocks into a joint brokerage account that she and her husband, Bill, own in both their names. The stocks in the brokerage account were bought with income earned from both of their jobs (community property). The one hundred shares of stock, now deposited in their joint account, commingles with the community property in the brokerage account and becomes indistinguishable from it. The AT&T stock now becomes community property. Ellie and Bill each own 50% of everything in the joint brokerage account.

Here are some examples of community property:

➡ You and your spouse own a home in Texas. You bought it with income that you earned and the deed states that you both own it as "husband and wife." It is community property, because you bought it with community property income (employment income earned by either spouse during a marriage) and the deed states that it is owned as husband and wife. You and your spouse each own 50% of the house.

➡ You and your spouse live in California. Your father bought you a speedboat before you were married, which you still own. You and your spouse opened a marina five years ago with your old boat being one of the six boats you both use to transport tourists to a nearby island. The marina and the five new boats were purchased with income earned during the marriage. You are both self-employed at the marina, where you carry people and goods on the boats and maintain and insure the boats and the real estate under one policy. The speedboat is now community property. It started out as separate property (property owned by one spouse before marriage), but it has become so commingled or mixed with community property that it has, itself, become community property. The marina and the five new boats are also community property, since they were bought with income earned in the early years of your marriage. Each spouse owns 50% of the marina and the six boats.

Separate Property in Community Property States

In community property states, separate property stays separate unless it commingles with community property, in which case it turns into community property. Separate property consists of the following:

➡ all property acquired prior to the marriage
➡ all property acquired following a legal separation but preceding the official divorce decree
➡ all income earned from previously owned property, but only if the spouse who earned it keeps it separate and it is not commingled with other income (This is only in Arizona, Nevada, New Mexico, and Washington. Wisconsin statute is unclear, so see an attorney if the law in this state affects you. In all other states it is community property.)
➡ all gifts received during marriage, if specifically given to only one spouse
➡ all inheritances received during marriage, if specifically given to only one spouse
➡ all property that started out as community property but is voluntarily converted into separate property by gift or agreement (Some states require this in writing. I recommend that *everyone* get this in writing.)

➡ certain federal pension programs, including Social Security and Railroad Retirement

Here are a few examples of separate property:

➡ You and your spouse live in New Mexico, a community property state. Your mother gave you a very expensive telescope for your 50th birthday. The telescope is separate property since it is a gift that was specifically given to you on a special occasion.

➡ You and your spouse own a house in Nevada, bought with both of your earnings and in the deed as "husband and wife." The house is community property. You discovered five years ago that you were seriously ill, and, wanting to avoid probate, you legally transferred your one-half ownership of the house to your spouse alone. The house is the separate property of your spouse now, since both of you voluntarily agreed in writing to give total ownership to your spouse.

Distinguishing Between Community Property and Separate Property

It is usually quite easy to determine what is community property and what is separate property. Sometimes, however, it becomes complicated and requires legal expertise to interpret state court decisions on the fine points of the differences. The following areas are potential problems and may require the help of a lawyer.

Businesses

If a business was owned by one spouse prior to the marriage, you need to figure out what proportion of the increased value of the business is community or separate property. Even if the value of the business decreased, the other spouse may still have acquired an ownership interest by investing time or money in the business.

State laws usually look at it this way: If both spouses work in the business, then any increase in value is community property. On the other hand, if only the original spouse works in it, it is often not clear whether the increased value is due to the contribution of the spouse that married into the business (community property), or whether the business would have succeeded just as well under the spouse who originally owned the business (separate property).

Serious problems involve businesses whose increase in value is due to both factors. If you possibly can, resolve the problem and write down your mutual agreement in a marital property agreement. If you and your spouse disagree about who owns what proportion of the business, see a lawyer now.

Appreciated Property

In most community property states, when separate property appreciates in value it remains separate property. If one spouse owned the property before marriage, but both spouses contribute to the maintenance and upkeep during marriage through community funds (mortgage, insurance, and upkeep), determining what percentage of the property remains separate property can be difficult. Again, this makes no difference if the surviving spouse inherits the property. Problems arise only when the property is left to someone else.

Personal Injury Awards

This type of property is difficult to characterize since it depends so much on the state in which you live. Some states treat it as separate property. Other states treat it one way while you are alive and another way when you are dead. The determining factor may be whether the other spouse caused the injury.

If a significant amount of your estate comes from a personal injury award or settlement and you and your spouse cannot agree, then you really must see a lawyer. You might also consider seeing a therapist or family counselor, especially if the other spouse caused the injury. These professionals cost less than a divorce lawyer.

Debts

The line between individual and community debts is frequently far from clear. Generally, a spouse's debt for food, clothing, and shelter is repaid from community property. A personal debt is the responsibility of the spouse who incurred it. Defining a necessity of life often involves consideration of court decisions and the impartiality of a third party.

Prenuptial Agreements or Marital Property Contracts

A prenuptial agreement is signed *prior* to marriage, while a marital property agreement is signed *after* a couple is already married. These agreements are valid contracts between you and your spouse defining how your assets are to be distributed at death or in the event of a divorce. If either of you doesn't like the way your state law defines ownership, you can jointly agree to change it.

Agreements of this sort have increased in all age groups, although the rise has been the greatest for older couples with children and assets from a former marriage, for whom the harsh realities of divorce and death are not abstract concepts. Concern about long-term care is also on the rise. For individuals who have built up separate estates over the years, there is justifiable concern that if one spouse goes into a nursing home or other facility for long-term care, it could impoverish the new spouse. Married couples, therefore, often sign a contract keeping separate property separate or making community property separate.

These agreements must comply with state law. This usually means that they must be in writing, voluntarily agreed to by both parties after full and fair disclosure of property ownership and financial obligations, and signed by both parties. The agreement sets forth both parties' decisions and is usually enforceable.

Tip: A judge will void a prenuptial agreement or a marital property agreement if he decides it is unfair, with one spouse taking advantage of the other spouse. A thread running through the law makes clear that courts want a spouse to be provided for in death and divorce. This common theme is found in community property states as well as common law states. While preventing injustice is the ideal standard, many spouses would agree that the standard does not always, unfortunately, determine the outcome.

Common Law States

All states and the District of Columbia, *with the exception of* Arizona, California, Idaho, Nevada, New Mexico, Texas, Washington, and Wisconsin (and Louisiana, which I am discounting), which are community property states, are common law states.

Separate Property in Common Law States

In common law states, the spouse who earns the money or acquires the property owns it separately and outright. This is the case unless the spouse transfers the proceeds into a type of shared ownership, like tenancy by the entirety. The most common indicator of ownership, whether you are married or not, *is whose name is on the title.* The property you own separately consists of:

⟹ all property you bought with your separate income or separate property; and

⟹ all property you own outright and separately in your name, as designated by title, deed, or any other legal ownership document.

If *you* inherit or earn money with which you buy a house, and title is taken in your and your spouse's name, both of you own the house. If *your* money buys the house and you put only your spouse's name on the deed, *your spouse owns the house.*

Here is an example of separate property in a common law state:

⟹ Bob and Terry live in Georgia (a common law state) in a house that Terry bought from the proceeds of a bonus she earned at her Wall Street investment banking firm (separate property). Terry puts the deed and title to the house in Bob's name as an anniversary present. Bob now owns the house outright and separately, with all of the legal ownership documents in his name. The house is now Bob's separate property. Bob may dispose of the house during his lifetime or at his death. Even though Terry paid for the house with her separate property, she relinquished all ownership rights when she put the deed and title to the house in Bob's name. Bob is now the sole owner of the house they both live in.

Marital Property in Common Law States

In common law states, marital property is property that is *owned by both spouses.* It consists of:

⟹ all property held in both spouses' names;

⟹ all property that was purchased with income from either or both spouses and that is held in both spouses' names; and

⟹ all property that was purchased with proceeds from the sale of property and that is held in both spouses' names.

If the property has no title document (most items other than a house, boat, or stocks), the person whose money bought it owns it. If joint money bought the item, both spouses own the property.

Here are some examples of marital property in common law states:

➥ As in the example above, Terry and Bob live in Georgia in a house bought with the bonus money Terry received from her high-paying job. The money is Terry's separate property. Instead of putting title and deed to the house in Bob's name only, Terry has the ownership documents placed both in her *and* Bob's name. In this scenario, the house is marital property and both spouses own it.

➥ Barbara and Peter, who live in Minnesota, buy an expensive snow-blower with money from a joint savings account. The rule states that if joint money buys the item, both spouses own the property. Consequently, both Barbara and Peter own the snowblower. Neither spouse may independently dispose of the machinery without the consent of the other spouse. The snowblower is marital property in a common law state.

WHAT ARE YOU REQUIRED TO LEAVE YOUR SURVIVING SPOUSE?

In Community Property States

Each spouse has the right to leave his one-half of the community property and all of his separate property to whomever he chooses.

In Common Law States

These states protect a surviving spouse against receiving less than his statutory share of an estate. *A spouse can't be disinherited. These states give surviving spouses a legal right to claim a certain percentage of the deceased spouse's estate. Most states grant the surviving spouse a legal right to one-third to one-half of the property left by the other.* The exact amount depends on whether there are children from the marriage.

If the prescribed amount is not given under the will, the surviving spouse is granted the "right of election" against the existing will (which I will explain in a moment). Percentages required by the different states are listed below.

In some states, the surviving spouse must inherit a percentage of the property that is transferred by will. Other states are going along with the current trend, which is that all property transferred by other means such as living trusts, jointly owned property, and insurance benefits must be included when calculating the minimum legal share that the surviving spouse is entitled to inherit. The value of nonfinancial items is determined by an appraiser at the spouse's request. All property, not just the property left by will, is called the "augmented estate."

What happens if a person leaves either nothing to a spouse or less than the spouse is entitled to under state law? The surviving spouse has the choice of either taking what was provided or rejecting it and instead taking the minimum share allowed by state law. Taking the share permitted by law is called "electing to take against the will." This amount doesn't automatically come to the surviving spouse. He must go to court and ask for it.

If the surviving spouse elects to take against the will, where do these assets come from? They are taken out of one or more gifts given to others by the will, often resulting in the inheritance to others being seriously reduced.

Required Percentages in Common Law States

The surviving spouse receives a right to one-third of the deceased spouse's real property (aka real estate) for life in Connecticut, Kentucky, Rhode Island, and South Carolina.

The surviving spouse receives a fixed percentage of the deceased spouse's estate in the following states:

Alabama	one-third of the augmented estate
Alaska	one-third of the augmented estate
Colorado	one-half of the augmented estate
District of Columbia	one-half of the estate
Florida	30% of the estate
Hawaii	one-third of the estate
Iowa	one-third of the estate
Maine	one-third of the augmented estate
Minnesota	one-third of the estate
Montana	one-third of the augmented estate
Nebraska	one-third of the augmented estate

New Jersey	one-third of the augmented estate
North Dakota	one-third of the augmented estate
Oregon	one-quarter of the estate
Pennsylvania	one-third of the estate
South Carolina	one-third of the estate
South Dakota	one-third of the augmented estate
Tennessee	one-third of the estate
Utah	one-third of the estate

The percentage to the surviving spouse varies in the following nineteen states if there are children. It is usually one-half to the spouse if there are no children and one-third to the spouse if there are children.

Arkansas	Michigan	Ohio
Illinois	Mississippi	Oklahoma
Indiana	Missouri	Vermont
Kansas	New Hampshire	Virginia
Maryland	New York	West Virginia
Massachusetts	North Carolina	Wyoming

Delaware's law is different from all of the above.

Delaware	$20,000 or one-third of the estate (whichever is less)

You are free to dispense with the balance of your estate in any manner you so choose, unless:

➡ you have designated other beneficiaries, as in life insurance contracts, retirement plans, or pay-on-death bank accounts;
➡ your property is restricted by contract, as in a partnership agreement;
➡ you have arranged to transfer property by joint tenancy, living trust, or other nonprobate estate planning methods.

If you want to leave your spouse little or nothing and you don't have your spouse's voluntary and written consent to your new property allocation, please see a lawyer. If you don't, your estate will be on a collision course with legal chaos.

MOVING TO A DIFFERENT STATE

Generally speaking, a will that is valid in one state is valid in another state. However, certain problems can occur if you move from a community property state to a common law state or vice versa. If you move within the same property ownership system (from one community property state to another community property state, or the same within the common law state system), there are no marital ownership problems.

Moving from a Community Property State to a Common Law State

When a married couple moves from a community property state to a common law state, each spouse generally retains a one-half interest in the property accumulated during their marriage.

Moving from a Common Law State to a Community Property State

Most of the community property states recognize your property according to the rules of the common law state in which you used to live.

➤ If you move from New Jersey (a common law state) to Texas (a community property state), Texas will enforce the rules of New Jersey. Common law rules will govern and the surviving spouse has a right to inherit one-third of the augmented estate.

Be aware of *three exceptions* to the rule above: California, Idaho, and Washington (all community property states) treat the previously acquired property as if it had been acquired in a community property state.

➤ If you move from Massachusetts (a common law state) to California, Idaho, or Washington (all community property states), *all* of your property will be treated according to community property rules. The surviving spouse will automatically inherit one-half of all earned or acquired property during the marriage—except for the property received as separate property by the deceased spouse either through gift or inheritance.

You are well on your way toward leaving your estate in an orderly fashion. Orderly estates do not attract lawyers. There is no money in them. You now know whether you are considered married for estate planning purposes. You also know whether you live in a community property state or a common law state, and, therefore, what you actually own and can thus give away. Finally, based on your resident state, you are aware of what (if anything) you absolutely must leave to your surviving spouse—like it or not! You will be putting these concepts to use in the next chapter when you make an inventory of your property.

3

Inventory Your Property

There is a perception increasingly shared by laypeople, but also by lawyers, that the gulf between the law and common sense has opened up in this crisis [the Clinton impeachment troubles] to a considerable degree. And that has caused people to lose confidence in the law.

—Anthony T. Kronman,
Dean of Yale Law School (1998)

Before you can decide who gets *what,* you must be completely sure of what the *what* is (i.e., your property) that you can give away. You can't give away what you don't own. To plan an estate, you must first determine the content and the value. Not only is the identity and cost of assets important, but where they are located can be equally significant. Assets not readily identifiable, such as those held in safe-deposit boxes or foreign bank accounts, may be lost forever.

Thorough estate planning requires a written inventory of your property in order to:

1. determine what you own;
2. determine how much of it you own;
3. determine where it is;
4. have a checklist of your property in front of you to easily match asset with beneficiary;
5. estimate the net value of your estate to determine whether your estate will be liable for federal estate taxes when you die (federal estate taxes begin for an individual's net estate worth $675,000 in 2000 and 2001, $700,000 in 2002 and 2003, $850,000 in 2004, $950,000 in 2005, and $1,000,000 in 2006 and thereafter; see chapter 13 for more on the federal estate tax exemption);
6. determine how much you owe in taxes and general debts;

7. gather your assets together in an orderly fashion in the event you want to consult with a lawyer;
8. determine whether there will be enough cash or other liquid assets to pay federal and state estate taxes as well as any unpaid income taxes, administration expenses, and funeral expenses; and
9. examine the assets and determine whether they will generate sufficient income to support your dependents or whether the purchase of additional life insurance should be considered.

TYPES OF PROPERTY

You will be dealing with two types of property. There is personal property, more informally known as personal possessions, which consists of everything you own except real estate. This includes assets such as cash, checking accounts, savings accounts, stocks, bonds, mutual funds, cars, jewelry, silver, coin collections, appliances, household furnishings, clothes, rugs, tools, and business property (not business real estate), plus intellectual property such as copyrights, patents, trademarks, and all other non–real estate possessions you own.

The second kind of property is real property (in legalese) or real estate (in plain English). This includes agricultural land, marina dock space, condos, co-ops, houses, mobile homes, time-shares, and undeveloped land.

THE INVENTORY WORKSHEET

An inventory worksheet will help you organize your property for easy reference. Determining your net worth is the first step in preparing an estate plan. You will accomplish this with:

1. a description of your assets and their location;
2. a determination of how your property is owned (individual, tenancy in common, joint tenancy with right of survivorship, tenancy by the entirety);
3. a determination of the percentage of the shared property that you own;
4. liabilities and debts.

It is up to you to decide if you want to itemize your property in a detailed fashion or you want to estimate your estate in an overall, general manner. If you want to leave all of your property to one person or if you are positive that your net worth is well under the federal estate tax threshold, there is less need for you to specify all major items of property. For everyone else, itemizing in some detail becomes necessary. Use whichever approach is helpful to you.

How to Inventory Your Property

Column 1—List Your Assets and Their Location

Make four columns on a piece of paper. In Column 1, list all of your property, personal possessions, and real estate, and note where each piece is located. There is nothing magical about the words you use and no legal language is necessary. Your only goal is to be clear about the property you own so that when the will is signed, there will be no question as to what you meant.

Liquid Assets

Liquid assets include cash, checking accounts, saving accounts, certificates of deposit, money market accounts, mutual funds, trust income. You can list accounts in any way that makes them easily identifiable. Account numbers should be included, if possible. Here are two examples:

➡ Checking account #28-85642-1187 at Chase Manhattan Bank, Rockefeller Center Branch, New York, NY (Robert E. Cook)
➡ Fidelity investment account #48-128367 (Joy W. Hecht), tel. (212) 282-4103

Other Personal Property

This includes all of your property *except* liquid assets, business interests, and real estate, but *including* stocks and bonds; automobiles and other vehicles; household goods; artwork and antiques; money owed you; livestock; vested interest in retirement plans, IRAs, death benefits, and annuities; and so on.

Personal possessions can be divided between specific items of value listed separately and those of lesser value listed in a group. This is the catchall category.

ITEMS OF GREATER VALUE
➡ my 1996 Ford automobile, license #874 4354 (Connecticut)
➡ my stamp collection in four leather albums (usually kept in the bookcase next to the television)
➡ all stocks and any other assets in account #283114— PaineWebber, Inc., Lafayette Street, San Francisco, California
➡ my Navajo rug, valued at approximately $3,000, hanging on my living-room wall in Junction City, Oregon

ITEMS OF LESSER VALUE
➡ all of my gardening tools [items in one category]
or
➡ all of my personal possessions and contents of my house [group of catchall items written this way especially if all of these items are going to one individual]

Business Personal Property
This includes business ownerships, miscellaneous receivables, patents, trademarks, royalties, and copyrights. A copyright should be identified by referring to the title of the copyrighted material, while a patent is identified by a patent number.

➡ my business—Desert Flour Bakery (Sarasota, Florida)
➡ patent #3,444,1412 for automatic dishwasher unloader
➡ all my copyrights and royalties in my book, *How to Die Without a Lawyer,* St. Martin's Press
➡ my partnership interest in the Chatty Chicken Restaurant, Prescott, Arizona
➡ all my shares of Y2K Corporation

Tips: Just because you own an interest in a shared business does not necessarily mean that you can dispose of your interest as you wish. The co-owners may have buyout, ownership, or management rights that must be considered. Therefore, check your documents to see if any restrictions exist on your right to transfer your interest at death.

Real Estate

For this category you should include addresses and descriptions of your property. Simply list the address, or, with undeveloped land, describe the property in normal language. You don't need to use the legal description found on the deed.

➡ 100 Weeburn Drive, Framingham, Massachusetts
➡ my lot on the northeast corner of Palisades Drive and 75th Street, Princeton, New Jersey

Sometimes real estate contains personal property. If you plan to leave these items together as one unit, specify this intent in your description. Specify the larger item first and refer to the rest as "personal property."

➡ my one-hundred-acre farm in Walpole, New Hampshire, with all tools, animals, machines, and other personal property located there
➡ my ownership of the mobile home at Sun-Up Mobile Home Community in Burlington, Vermont, and all possessions, furnishings, and personal property found therein

Column 2—State How Your Property Is Owned—If Ownership of That Item Is Shared, Enter the Type of Shared Ownership

You need be concerned with Columns 2 and 3 only if (1) you own property with someone else, or (2) you are married and live in a community property state. If you own all of your property yourself, and you are not married and living in a community property state, then skip to Column 4. (See chapter 2 to refresh your memory on community property states and common law states.)

For any property that you own with someone else, you must determine what share of it you own so you will know what is yours to give away. You may be aware of your ownership of property with others, but you may not be aware of how you and the other owner(s) hold legal title to the property. Never guess. Take the time to find out. Locate the deed to the house, the stock certificates, or the title to the automobile to ascertain whether you own them independently or whether you and your spouse own them in joint tenancy. The county property recorder's office can give you information about real estate records.

Once you have this information, make a second column, Column 2, and state how you own the property (individually or jointly), corresponding to the particular asset in Column 1. Below is a summary of the different kinds of ownership. Note that only the first one, individual ownership (I.O.), is owned by you outright. On your worksheet, in Column 2, indicate the kind of ownership by the abbreviations given below. If you need to do some research, just indicate that the property is jointly owned for the time being. You can come back to it later when you have more information.

Property You *Can* Leave by Will

Individual Ownership (I.O.)

You are the sole owner. You do not share ownership and you are not married in a community property state. For purposes of making your will, you are the outright owner even if a lender, as is true with car notes and mortgages, has some legal ownership in that property until you pay off the loan.

➡ *In common law states,* all property in your name is owned by you individually, solely, and outright.

Community Property in a Community Property State (C.P.)

Virtually all property acquired by a married couple during their marriage, while they reside in a community property state, is community property. Each of the marriage partners owns one-half thereof. You may leave *your one-half* of the community property to anyone you choose. The *other one-half* belongs to the other spouse. You have no basis for mentioning your spouse's one-half in your will because you don't own it.

If you and your spouse are unsure about whether something is separate or community property, you can settle the matter by jointly characterizing this property in either one of the two ownership categories, in writing, signed by both of you. Get legal help (or therapy) if you can't agree on the characterization of the property. I suggest trying therapy first. It's cheaper.

Separate Property in a Community Property State (S.P.)

In community property states (Arizona, California, Idaho, Nevada, New Mexico, Texas, Washington, and Wisconsin), all property that isn't community property is separate property.

In community property states, a spouse's separate property is:

➡ all property acquired prior to marriage;

➡ income earned from previously owned property, if the spouse who earned it keeps it separate—except in Washington, where this type of income is always community property;

➡ gifts or inheritances received during marriage, if directed to only one spouse (wedding gifts are community property);

➡ property that, despite originally being classified as community property, is converted into separate property by gift or agreement, which must be in writing; and

➡ property acquired after a legal separation.

Tenancy in Common (T.C.)

Tenancy in common is the most common way for unmarried people to own property together. Parents often leave their children property in this manner. Tenancy in common is property you own with someone but the ownership document doesn't specify any type of shared ownership such as joint tenancy or tenancy by the entirety. (See the first three sections under "Property You *Cannot* Leave by Will" below for a full explanation of the joint ownership of property.) Married couples can also use this form of joint ownership, but more often they use other forms of co-ownership.

Each co-owner is permitted to transfer his share independently. Thus, when one tenant dies, his interest goes into his estate to pass as that tenant so desires. An advantage of this form of joint tenancy is that it can be transferred by will or to a living trust, which will avoid probate, yet provide a survivorship feature.

Property You *Cannot* Leave by Will

Joint Tenancy for Real Estate (J.T.)

Joint tenancy must be created by a written document. A joint tenancy exists when the ownership deed *specifies* that it is held in joint tenancy. It is frequently abbreviated as JTWRS, which stands for "joint tenancy with right of survivorship."

The right of survivorship means that when one of the joint tenants dies, his share automatically goes to the surviving owner(s) in equal amounts. The interest in the deceased property does *not* go into his estate. Therefore, a joint tenant cannot leave his share of joint tenancy property to someone else, even if a will or living trust directs to the contrary. The deed supersedes.

Joint Tenancy for Personal Property (J.T.P.P.)

Joint tenancy for personal property, unlike joint tenancy for real estate, can be created without documents of title. All you have to do is declare in an acknowledged written document that you and the co-owner own the property "in joint tenancy" or "as joint tenants." When one of the owners dies, his share automatically transfers to the surviving owner. It cannot go into a will or living trust.

STATES THAT HAVE RESTRICTED OR
ABOLISHED JOINT PROPERTY

If you live in one of these states and you have a joint tenancy ownership document, check with a lawyer to see what you have now as a result of the changes.

➡ Alaska—No joint tenancy in real estate, except for husband and wife.
➡ Pennsylvania—Statute allows no joint tenancy in real estate. Courts, however, have allowed joint tenancy with right of survivorship, when it has been created by the explicit words of a deed, "joint tenancy with right of survivorship" or JTWRS.
➡ Tennessee—No joint tenancy in any property, except for married couples.
➡ Texas—No joint tenancy for any property, unless there is a separate written agreement between joint owners. This agreement is in addition to the other specific words that must appear in the deed, JTWRS.

Tenancy by the Entirety (T.E.)

In earlier years, a husband and wife were considered to be one entity. What was his was his and what was *hers* was his! Times have changed. Tenancy by the entirety has been abolished in more than one-half of the states. For those states that still allow it, there is tenancy by the entirety for both real estate and personal possessions.

This form of ownership is basically the same as joint tenancy with right of survivorship except that it is *limited exclusively to married couples*. Like JTWRS, the words "tenants by the entirety" or "tenancy by the entirety" *must* appear in the deed, in writing. *When one spouse dies, his share automatically goes to the surviving spouse.* It cannot be included in a will, since the spouse beneficiary is predetermined. Tenancy by the entirety may be changed to some other form of property ownership, but only if both spouses agree to the change in writing.

STATES WITH TENANCY BY THE ENTIRETY OWNERSHIP

Alaska*	Maryland	Ohio
Arkansas	Massachusetts	Oklahoma
Delaware	Michigan*	Oregon*
District of Columbia	Mississippi	Pennsylvania
Florida	Missouri	Tennessee
Hawaii	New Jersey*	Vermont
Indiana*	New York*	Virginia
Kentucky*	North Carolina*	Wyoming*

Living Trust Property (L.T.)

This is property that has already been transferred to a living trust. It cannot be transferred by will unless you, the creator of the living trust, have terminated the living trust.

Community Property (C.P.)

In community property states, any property that a spouse earns or acquires during a marriage is shared community property. Even if only one spouse's name is on the title document, it is still community property if it was bought with money during the marriage. As discussed above, separate property in a community property state or your one-half share of community property can be left to whomever you choose. The one-half that belongs to your spouse cannot be transferred by will or living trust since it doesn't belong to you.

*Allows tenancy by the entirety only for real estate.

Community property that *cannot* be transferred by will consists of:

➡ income from work performed by either spouse during marriage;
➡ property and earnings acquired from community income;
➡ gifts made to both spouses;
➡ property that, despite originally being classified as separate property, is deliberately turned into community property by the spouses; and
➡ separate property that is so mixed up with community property (commingled) that one is no longer distinguishable from the other. When this happens, the separate property becomes community property. Commingling can occur when income from separate property is put in a shared bank account, for example.

Community Property with Right of Survivorship (C.P.R.S.)

This is community property that functions like joint property. The surviving spouse *automatically* inherits the one-half previously owned by the deceased spouse. This form of ownership is available in Arizona, Nevada, Texas, and Wisconsin.

Insurance Policies, Pensions, and Retirement Accounts (I.P.R.)

Insurance policies, pensions, and retirement accounts, such as an IRA or a 401(k) plan, with an already named beneficiary, cannot be left by will.

Tip: When estimating the size of an estate for tax purposes, remember that the value of the life insurance policy is the face value, the payout, of the policy.

Property Registered in Transfer-on-Death Forms (T.D.)

More than one-half of states now allow stocks and bonds to be held in transfer-on-death forms, with already named beneficiaries to receive the securities at the owner's death.

Joint Tenancy Bank Accounts (J.T.B.A.)

Most forms of bank accounts can be owned in joint tenancy, including checking, savings, and certificates of deposits. To open such an

account, everyone involved signs as joint tenants with right of survivorship and all tenants have access to the account. When one joint tenant
dies, the surviving tenant(s) is the beneficiary, making these accounts
impossible to be transferred by will or living trust.

Totten Trusts (T.T.)

A Totten trust is a joint bank account to which your co-owner has
no rights *during your lifetime*. The joint owner becomes the beneficiary
and is entitled to the funds *only after your death*.

Column 3—List Your Percentage of the Shared Property

In Column 3, list the percentage of each item of shared property that
you own. People who own property as tenants in common or in partnerships or corporations should be extremely careful. It is possible to
own *any percentage* of the property (1% to 99%), so check the document to find out your percentage of the pie.

If you are the sole owner, your portion is, of course, 100%.

If the property is community property or tenancy by the entirety, the
ownership is automatically split fifty-fifty. You own 50%. Your spouse
owns 50%.

If the property is held in joint tenancy with right of survivorship, all
of the joint tenants own equal shares. Therefore, if there are two owners, each owner owns 50%. If there are three owners, each owner owns
33.3%. If there are four owners, each owner owns 25%. And so on.

Column 4—Estimate the Current Net Value of Your Ownership

In Column 4, enter an estimate of the net value of each item of property, which means your equity in your share of the property. Equity is
the market value of your share, minus your share of any debts on it,
such as a mortgage, home equity loan, past due taxes, liens on the
house, or the loan amount due on a car.

This evaluation is only an estimate. You do not need to get apprais-
ers to arrive at exact figures. The value of your estate will undoubtedly
change by the time you die. The net worth of your property and the

death taxes your estate will pay are based on the value of your property when you die, not on its current value. What you need here are rough estimates. *Some research might be beneficial* to determine how much a house in your neighborhood just sold for or how much the man at the used car lot down the street would give you for that 1983 Chevy.

How to Determine the Net Worth of Your Home:

Example: Matthys owns a house with a market value of $300,000 as a tenant in common with wife, Mary Ann. Each of them owns one-half of the property. Matthys proceeds to figure out the net value of his share by subtracting his mortgage, his home equity loan, and some back property taxes that had slipped his mind from the market value of the house, to arrive at his total equity in the property.

market value of house	$300,000
owed on mortgage	$100,000
home equity loan	$ 40,000
back property taxes due	$ 2,000
total equity ($300,000	$158,000
minus $142,000)	
net worth of Matthys' share	$ 79,000
($158,000 divided by 2 because	
they each own one-half of the	
property as tenants in common)	

Total Assets: Now, add up the net value of all your assets and write that figure down at the bottom of Column 4.

List Your Liabilities

Now list any liabilities (debts) that have not been dealt with previously. This list is separate from Column 4. You have already accounted for the mortgage on your real estate and the loan on your car, so you don't have to list these. What you do need to list, however, is all *major liabilities* (not the small stuff that keeps changing anyway, like monthly credit card payments and the electricity bill) *not accounted for,* so that you can get a clearer picture of your net worth. What you need to account for here are debts like a $5,000 loan from a friend, school loans, home improvement loans, and federal and state taxes—past and currently due.

Total Liabilities: Now, add up the estimate of all your liabilities and write that amount at the bottom of Column 4, below "Total Assets."

You're almost finished. Stay with me here.

Your Net Worth

In the last step of this exercise, you estimate your current net worth. To arrive at this figure, you will simply subtract your total liabilities from your total assets. The difference between these two amounts is your net worth.

————————

Congratulations! I recognize how tedious this task can be, especially if you did a thorough written inventory of all your property. You now have a clear idea of what you can leave to others and also a general idea of where you stand on the estate tax exemption issue. The time and thought you put into this inventory will benefit you in the long run by making other aspects of your estate planning a lot easier and more complete. With knowledge in hand of what you are permitted to give away at your death, you are ready for the more pleasurable undertaking of naming the beneficiaries of this property.

4

Choosing Your Beneficiaries

I leave to my banker, Mr. John Levy, the sum of 2,000 pounds, provided that, within three monthes of my death, he walks the length of Bond Street, at midday and not on a Saturday or a Sunday, dressed in women's clothing, which should give him an inkling of the feelings to which he subjected me before advancing me a loan.

—from the will of Jackson E. Negilski

It's your money and with very few exceptions you are free to do what you want with it. Deciding which persons or organizations you choose to receive your property is obviously the main focus of an estate plan.

This chapter describes those who will receive the benefits of your estate—your beneficiaries. Beneficiaries can be members of your immediate family, charities, friends, trusts, relatives, and organizations. Your beneficiaries can receive their inheritance either outright or in trust. Gifts can be made in a dollar amount or as a percentage of the estate. Gifts can also be shared.

You will learn about not only the kinds of beneficiaries who can inherit, but also important information about the forgiving of debts, the naming of beneficiaries outside the United States, the disinheriting of spouses and children, pets as beneficiaries, and restrictions on gift giving.

You may know who your major beneficiaries will be, particularly if you are leaving all of your assets to only one person or to just a couple of persons. But wait a minute! Even so, check to be sure there are no pieces of property, special or sentimental items, that you might like to leave to specific beneficiaries. Perhaps there is an old photo album of sporting events that would have special meaning to a high school buddy or a specific piece of jewelry that your best friend has always admired (especially if you have only sons). A considerate friend of mine is leaving me a painting we both admired in an art gallery. She subsequently purchased the painting. Take the time to jog your memory by walking through the house and garage. With a little time and effort you can bring joy with the proper remembrance. Therefore, even if you think you know what you want to do, read on, for this chapter covers important information that everyone should take into account.

There is no reason to hire a lawyer to help you name your beneficiaries. First of all, only *you* know the individuals that you want to inherit your lifetime accumulation. No one can decide this for you. Second, no law degree is required to write names down in plain English. Just use the names by which these individuals are known. If someone marries, divorces, takes back their maiden name, or changes their name in a Hindu ashram, there is no reason to change your will or trust. The individual with the new name, as well as other concerned parties, will know who you had in mind.

TYPES OF BENEFICIARIES

There are different types of beneficiaries. Here is a list of the major ones:

1. Primary beneficiaries—Those to whom you leave specific gifts.
2. Alternate beneficiaries—Those to whom the gift goes in the event that the primary beneficiary dies before you do.
3. Life estate beneficiaries—Those who have no legal ownership in the property, but instead have a "life estate" interest in it. They have the right to receive income from or to use the property during their lifetime. They have *no right,* however, to leave the property to anyone during their lifetime or at their death.
4. Final beneficiaries—Those named to inherit the property with all its rights and responsibilities after the life estate beneficiary dies.
5. Residuary beneficiaries—Those persons or organizations that will receive the balance or remainder of the property not specifically given to someone else. If the primary or alternate

beneficiaries predecease you, the residuary beneficiaries inherit the specific property.

6. Two or more beneficiaries sharing ownership of the property—Each beneficiary receives a portion of the ownership of the property. Some people like to leave shared gifts, especially to their children.

PRIMARY BENEFICIARIES

Primary beneficiaries are the ones named to receive specific items of property. Some people name many primary beneficiaries to inherit specific items of property. Some name none at all, leaving all of their property to the residuary beneficiary.

➡ I leave my gold watch to my friend, Carolyn L. Hughes.
➡ I leave my house on Peck Street to my friends, Wendy and Louis Clark.

Minors or Young Adult Beneficiaries

When minors (anyone under 18 years of age in all states except for Georgia where it is under 14 years of age and Wyoming where it is under 19) are named as primary beneficiaries, they can technically receive the property outright or in trust. *However, a minor can only own a small amount of property outright. The amount is determined by state law and ranges from $2,500 to $5,000. If a minor owns property above the designated amount, it must be legally controlled and supervised by an adult, known as a guardian of the property. You can designate this guardian of the property to manage the minor's property until he reaches majority. If you do not designate a guardian, one will be appointed by the court.* It is obviously preferable for *you* to appoint someone you know and trust, rather than for the court to appoint a stranger. The guardian will manage the inheritance subject to whatever restrictions you place on the gift. (See chapter 5 for a full chapter on leaving property to minors and young adults.)

A young adult beneficiary is defined here as someone between ages 18 to 35. Although legally an adult, you may want some adult management if your children fall within this age group.

Restrictions on Gifts to Primary Beneficiaries

The law places some restrictions on giving. Most people leave gifts out-right to friends, family, or organizations. Some people, however, want to effectively control from the grave. Such behavior is not always allowed. There are some restrictions and conditions that are prohibited:

The individual who causes the death of the person who wrote the will or the trust cannot inherit under it. Or, as a New York court once proclaimed, "No man shall be permitted to profit by his own wrong."

➡ Janie and Bud have been business partners for years. Bud be-comes ill, decides to get his affairs in order, and executes his will leav-ing his one-half of the business to Janie. Janie, who has always had a gambling problem, falls behind in her payments to the casino. She gets roughed up once too often and realizes that the "collection agents" mean business. All of a sudden she sees the answer to her problem. She takes a gun out of Bud's desk drawer, shoots him, and places the gun in Bud's hand to make it look like a suicide. The police, however, are not fooled. Janie's fingerprints are all over the gun. Also, Janie makes the mistake of shooting Bud in the back of the head at twenty feet. Janie is convicted of murder. She doesn't inherit Bud's one-half of the business since it was she who caused his death. Janie goes to prison for life and Bud's portion of the business goes to his residuary beneficiary, Niketa, his massage therapist.

You *cannot* leave money for an illegal purpose.

➡ I leave an annual income of $100,000 to Marc Resnick if he es-tablishes Drug Dealers, Inc., an organization whose purpose it is to fa-cilitate cocaine smuggling into the United States.
➡ I leave my house to my friend, Julie Simpson, so long as she uses it to construct bombs to overthrow the United States government. If she ceases to use the house for this purpose, I then leave the house to the Daughters of the American Revolution.

You *cannot* leave property where the condition is *against public policy*. Public policy is not always easy to determine, as there are no of-ficial rules and reasonable people can disagree. What was against pub-lic policy fifty years ago is not necessarily against it today. One court has determined something as being against public policy if it "contravenes any established interest of society, or conflicts with the morals of the time, tends to injustice or oppression, restraint of liberty or legal rights."

➡ I leave $50,000 to Duncan Stalvey, who must use the money to fulfill his lifelong wish of keeping women pregnant, barefoot, and in the kitchen.

➡ I leave my house at 100 Easy Street to Mark Keitlen, but only if he uses it "to protect, finance, and support" the practice of wife beating.

You *cannot* attempt to *totally* restrain or prohibit the future marriage of a beneficiary.

➡ I leave my estate to my granddaughter, Alexa, provided she never marries.

A *partial restraint on marriage* that does not prohibit it altogether, but merely prohibits it under certain circumstances, is *usually* legal and upheld.

➡ I leave $50,000 to my granddaughter, Alexa, provided she does not marry before the age of 21, and provided she marries someone of South American extraction.

Although the courts are not totally consistent on *prohibitions against religious affiliations*, bequests that are subject to a condition that the beneficiary adhere to a particular religion, renounce it, or marry or refrain from marrying someone of a particular faith have generally been held to be legal and enforceable.

➡ I leave $10,000 to Andrew Miller, provided that he marries someone of the Jewish faith.

Some conditions can be very straightforward.

➡ I leave $50,000 to my son, James, if he graduates from a four-year college within six years of entering the institution.

Other conditions are limited only by your imagination. History reveals many uncommon conditions, such as those left by Jackson E. Negilski at the beginning of the chapter.

As the United States Supreme Court wrote in a case of a conditional bequest, "The right of a testator to attach to a gift in his Will any lawful terms he sees fit, no matter how whimsical or capricious, is widely, if not universally, recognized." Having said that, think twice before imposing restrictions and conditions on your gifts. They can be difficult to enforce and monitor, even if legal. It is very hard to do either one without an attorney. What might give you a moment or two of power and control could give your beneficiaries years of trouble at enormous expense. *Conditions and restrictions bring lawyers almost as much pleasure as a big probate estate.* Don't give them the satisfaction! Keep it simple.

In situations where the restriction is clearly illegal, the condition is unclear, or the condition fails to meet any of the other legal requirements, the restriction is void and the inheritance generally passes directly to the beneficiary *free* of the condition.

Tip: See a lawyer and set up a trust if you want to make a conditional gift. Someone must be responsible for making sure the conditions are fulfilled. The best way to accomplish this is to put the property in a trust and have the trust managed by a trustee.

Restrictions on Gifts to Charity

You may want to leave some of your money to a charity or to a public or private organization, like the American Cancer Society, the Knights of Columbus, or the University of Pennsylvania. You can leave property to any organization you choose, as long as it is not set up for some illegal purpose. The organization does not even need to have a nonprofit status, unless you want your gift to qualify for a charitable estate tax deduction.

While you can basically leave your property to whomever you choose, *there are a few remaining states that impose limitations on your ability to leave large percentages of your property to charities*. However, in these states that impose such limitations (District of Columbia, Florida, Georgia, Idaho, Montana, and Mississippi), they usually only apply if the deceased leaves a surviving spouse and/or children or grandchildren at his death. If there are no such direct heirs, the limitation will not apply and you can leave your entire estate to charity, if you wish to do so.

Laws limiting what you can leave to charities are holdovers from early England, where so much property was being acquired by the Church of England that the Crown became fearful of the tremendous power the Church was amassing. The accumulation of wealth under one roof was also regarded as contrary to economic growth and the well-being of the family. Both suffered when the Church, as it frequently did, promised a place in heaven for those approaching death if the Church were immediately and properly compensated.

If you live in one of these states, see a lawyer if you want to leave *more than one-half of your estate to a charity*. However, if you want to leave a relatively small percentage of your estate to charity, even if you live in one of these restricted states, you needn't be concerned.

ALTERNATE BENEFICIARIES

These are the people or organizations you name to receive a specific gift if the primary beneficiary dies before you do. You can name one alternate beneficiary or you can name multiple alternate beneficiaries.

➡ I leave my house to Lester Martin, or, if he dies before I do, to Ellen Skidmore.

➡ I leave the assets in my PaineWebber, Inc. account #23-67842 to Mary Martin, or, if she dies before I do, to her son, Ebony, and her daughter, Molly, in equal shares.

There is another way to handle the possibility that the primary beneficiary might die before you do. Instead of naming an alternate beneficiary, you can always modify your will or trust to name a new beneficiary if the primary beneficiary dies. If you fail to name an alternate beneficiary, the property will automatically go to the residuary beneficiary.

➡ Sam and Gladys have been married for forty years and have no children. Sam is leaving his entire estate to Gladys, with the exception of a collection of bird feeders that Fred has always admired. Sam is, therefore, leaving the bird feeders to Fred. Sam does not name an alternate beneficiary in the event that Fred dies before him. Fred *does* die and the bird feeders pass to the residuary beneficiary who is Gladys. Were Sam to have named an alternate beneficiary for the bird feeders, it would have been Gladys. Either way, Gladys inherits the feeders.

LIFE ESTATE BENEFICIARIES AND FINAL BENEFICIARIES

The life estate beneficiary receives only a limited interest in the property during his lifetime. He has the income or use of the property, but he may not dispose of the property. This interest ends when the life beneficiary dies. You specify the final beneficiary to inherit the property outright when the life estate beneficiary dies.

➡ Dave leaves his unmarried brother, Wand, a life interest in the income of certain stocks. Wand is the life estate beneficiary of the stocks. He can neither sell them nor leave them to anyone when he dies. Upon Wand's death, Betty H. Morgan inherits the stocks outright. She is the final beneficiary and can do with the stocks whatever she wishes.

Life estates are usually created by a trust in order to reduce or eliminate estate taxes or to impose controls over property. Drafting such a trust is more complicated than it may seem. Therefore, you need a lawyer. Think through the substance and the contingencies before you meet with the lawyer and you will cut some of the time and cost involved.

RESIDUARY BENEFICIARY

The residuary beneficiary is the person or organization that will inherit what remains of your property after the specific gifts are given and all debts, taxes, probate, administration fees, and attorney fees are paid. This is property that was not received by other beneficiaries, either because no one was specifically named to get the property or because the named beneficiary died before you did. Some people make no specific gifts, or very few of them, leaving all of their property to the residuary beneficiary.

➡ I leave my residuary estate to Cyndy Sheldon.

You can name more than one residuary beneficiary.

➡ I leave 25% of my residuary estate to Peg Duncan, 25% of my residuary estate to Lynn Becker, 25% of my residuary estate to Jennifer Hunter, and 25% of my residuary estate to the Elaine Harrison Children's Poetry Scholarship Fund at the University of Chicago.

ALTERNATE RESIDUARY BENEFICIARY

Even if you do not appoint alternate primary beneficiaries, it is a good idea to name an alternate residuary beneficiary.

➡ I leave my residuary estate to Jock Becker, or, if he does not survive me, to his son, Tom Becker.

You can name more than one alternate residuary beneficiary.

➡ I leave my residuary estate to Alice Allen, or, if she does not survive me, I leave 50% of my residuary estate to her daughter, Che Swanson, and 50% of my residuary estate to the Burmese Cat Humane Society.

TWO OR MORE BENEFICIARIES SHARING OWNERSHIP OF THE PROPERTY

Sometimes parents want to leave shared gifts to their children, especially real estate. Each of the beneficiaries inherits a portion of ownership of the property and all of the beneficiaries own the property itself.

➥ Barbara leaves her house in the Florida Keys to her three children, Andrew, Allie, and Sedona, in equal shares. Each owns an undivided one-third interest in the property.

There are several issues to consider before leaving your property to two or more beneficiaries. First, what percentage of ownership does each child receive? Equal shares are presumed but your intent should be specifically stated in your will. Second, what happens when one person wants to sell and if he does sell, who is he allowed to sell it to? Be specific or the lawyers will see you coming. Third, what happens if one beneficiary dies before you do? Alternate beneficiaries for shared ownership of a house can be complicated. Do you leave it to a friend of the other beneficiary, the spouse, or the surviving children?

Tip: If the beneficiaries did not get along while you were alive, there is no reason to believe they will get along when you are dead. If they did not amicably resolve conflicts in the past, why think they will do so in the future? Few people want to leave serious, costly conflicts to anyone, especially to their children.

Pets As Beneficiaries

Pets are an interesting estate planning challenge. For many owners, a pet is a person, a member of the family, not a piece of property (like a sofa or a lawn mower), which is the way the law sees your favored four-legged friend.

In Manhattan, the Association of the Bar of the City of New York publishes a brochure called *Providing for Your Pets in the Event of Your Death*. As its name suggests, the brochure explains how to leave instruction in your will for the care and well-being of what for many people is their best friend. The brochure, available upon request, provides several ways to establish a trust for pets by making a conditional bequest. The pet and a sum of money are left to a beneficiary with the condition that the money be spent for the care of the pet. This procedure, the brochure continues, can be disregarded by the courts and is not advisable. A better way is to *give* the pet and a sum of money to a friend with the *request* that the money be spent on caring for the animal.

Another possibility is to leave the pet to a friend (make sure they have agreed to this beforehand) and make an arrangement with a veterinarian. Based on the age and health of the animal, you and the vet can agree on a lump sum in exchange for lifetime care for the pet.

BENEFICIARIES OUTSIDE THE UNITED STATES

You can leave property to anyone living *outside of the United States*. It will be your executor's responsibility to make sure the beneficiary gets the property, just as it is the executor's responsibility to make sure the beneficiary gets the property if he lives *in the United States*.

If the property itself is located *outside* of the country (real estate is an obvious example), the situation is a bit different. The property, under these circumstances, must be transferred according to the laws of the country in which the property is located. For this, you need to see a lawyer. It cannot confidently be done by a will on your own.

FORGIVING A DEBT

Forgiving a debt is like giving a gift to your debtor. Any debt, whether oral or written, can be forgiven. This operates to release the individual responsible for the debt and has no income tax impact.

Tip: If the loan was given while you were married (especially if you live in a community property state), make sure that you have the power to forgive the debt. You may be able to forgive only one-half of the debt unless your spouse agrees in writing to forgive *his* one-half of the debt as well.

DISINHERITANCE

Your spouse and your children are the only ones to consider when you think about disinheriting someone. No one else has any automatic legal claim on your property, so no one else can be disinherited.

Disinheriting a Spouse

Every state has some provision that prevents one spouse from disinheriting another spouse. The law's intent is to prevent the surviving spouse from being financially ruined and to prevent him from becoming a ward of the state. A surviving spouse, therefore, is protected by the law and must receive part of the estate, even against your wishes and even if you don't include your spouse in your will. (See chapter 2 for discussion of the prohibition against disinheriting a surviving spouse.)

If you live in one of the common law states or the District of Columbia, the surviving spouse has the right to take one-third to one-half of the estate outright, even if a lesser amount is mentioned in the will. This prerogative of the surviving spouse is called the right of election.

If you live in one of the community property states, the laws themselves give the spouse a right to one-half of *all* the property acquired by both spouses during the marriage. Since one-half of the marital property *already belongs* to the surviving spouse, this spouse has no further legal right to inherit any more of the deceased spouse's property. In other words, what you already have under community property state law is all you are required to get.

Disinheriting a Child

All states allow you to disinherit a child, if you do so *expressly. You cannot disinherit a child simply by failing to mention him in your will.* If you do fail to do so, that child may have a legal right to claim part of your property. The reason these laws are in place is to protect a child from being unintentionally overlooked. This is not to say that a child must be as much as a primary beneficiary. He can be an alternate or residuary beneficiary. The point is, a child must be *mentioned* to at least knowledge that you are aware of his existence. No such rules apply to grandchildren.

Most wills require that you list all of your children and grandchildren. If you want to disinherit a child, your will could provide a few sentences such as: "I am not leaving property in this will to one or more of my children whom I have identified above. My decision is intentional, not accidental." There is no legal requirement that you give a reason for your decision, although you may do so if you wish.

Tip: Note that the language here is important. If a mistaken belief is actually stated in the will as the basis for the omission, then even though the omission was intentional and enforceable, thereby precluding the child from taking a share under the omitted-child rules, the child may *still* be able to void that portion of the will on the grounds of *mis-*

take. An example of this would be, "I am intentionally omitting my daughter, Kathy Ann, from my will because she ran away and I don't know where she is." If Kathy Ann shows up, very much alive, she could contest the disinheritance because the reason you gave for your decision to disinherit her was based on the *mistaken belief* that she was dead. Be careful with your reasons.

If you have another child after you have signed your will, you should prepare another will, list the child's name, and leave him property—or not—as you choose.

PERSONAL EXPRESSIONS

Explanations and personal commentaries to beneficiaries may be written into a will or living trust or they may be written in a separate letter accompanying the documents. Expressions are not legally binding. However, make sure that your words cannot possibly be misunderstood as making or modifying gifts already made in the documents. Also, unless the comments are short, it is better to write a separate letter and attach it to the will.

People write letters mostly to explain a disinheritance, to explain to children why property is left to them in unequal portions (special needs of one child, the fact that one child has previously been given money, etc.), or to seize the last opportunity to say things they were hesitant or afraid to say while they were alive.

It is wise, however, to be careful about making angry, sarcastic, and libelous statements (ones that are injurious to the reputation of another) in your will or trust. Your estate could be liable for damages. If you insist on saying something questionable, check it out with a lawyer. Loose writing can cost the estate thousands of dollars just to defend against such a claim. As they say in the Navy, "Loose lips sink ships." And this wouldn't even include the cost of the settlement.

UNMARRIED COUPLES

Unmarried couples living together have no legal right to inherit *any* of each other's property. However, each person is free to leave his property to anyone he chooses, including the person he is living with.

An agreement between unmarried couples living together that provides for specific rights of inheritance will usually be enforceable and is a wise step to take. Since it is becoming more common for unmarried people to live together for long periods, the rights of common law marriages are becoming more of a concern. Those who do not wish to share their estate with one another may find that upon one person's death, the period of time in which they cohabited may give rights to the surviving person that were not anticipated.

For example, in New Hampshire, if an unmarried couple live together "as husband and wife" for three years before the death of one of the partners, the other partner has rights to the estate of the deceased, similar to those of a surviving spouse. To avoid these and other complications that will inevitably require the services of a lawyer, an unmarried couple should have a written agreement that fixes their respective rights at death.

SIMULTANEOUS DEATH CLAUSE

The laws of most states provide that in the event of a common disaster, each of the persons involved is presumed to have survived the other. Therefore, if you and your spouse die in a common accident and it cannot be determined who died first, each of you will be deemed to have survived the other and your estates will be distributed accordingly.

PROPERTY THAT YOU INTEND TO LEAVE TO A BENEFICIARY BUT THAT YOU NO LONGER OWN AT YOUR DEATH

Specific Gifts

If you leave someone a specific piece of property—for example, the fourteen-karat-gold earrings with small clusters of diamonds—and it is no longer in your possession when you die (you gave them to your daughter-in-law before she married your only son), the beneficiary that you named in your will is simply out of luck. The gift is said "to adeem." The meaning of "adeem" is "to revoke or to take away." The gift to your daughter-in-law is valid and she gets to keep the earrings.

Cash Gifts

If you have cash gifts and there is not enough cash in the estate at the time of your death and you have not included specific instructions in your will about what the executor should do in the event of a cash shortfall, the state law on what is known as "abatement" takes over. The meaning of "abatement" is "to decrease." The state statute describes what to do when the one who wrote the will gives gifts that exceed the total amount available for distribution. Or, to put it another way, abatement is where the selfless wishes of the will maker outmatch the size of his paltry or insolvent estate.

Different states handle this problem differently. Some states dictate that cash first be taken from the residuary. Others provide for a pro rata decrease in cash gifts, preferably without the sale of property.

Residuary Option—Cash Is Taken from the Residuary

➡ Philip leaves $20,000 each to Picasso and Suki. When Philip dies, his estate has only $30,000 in cash. There is a shortfall of $10,000. However, he also owns property that he left to his residuary beneficiary. The residuary property must be sold in order to give Picasso and Suki their money. The residuary beneficiary takes what is left over.

Pro Rata Option—Decease in Cash Gifts, Preferably Without the Sale of Property

➡ Philip leaves $20,000 each to Picasso and Suki. When Philip dies, his estate has only $30,000 in cash. However, he also owns property that he left to his residuary beneficiary. That residuary property is not sold to make up the shortfall of $10,000. Picasso and Suki each inherit $15,000, dividing the available $30,000 in cash.

States vary as to the details, but these are the basic laws. You can choose which option your executor should use. If you do not put either choice in your will, state law will dictate the option required by that state.

Tip: Keep your will up-to-date. Whenever circumstances change, modify your will to accommodate the changes. It will save your beneficiaries time and money, as leaving more than you own can be complicated and will guarantee an influx of attorneys.

Determining what you own and who will inherit it are two necessary steps in making your will. An architect draws the blueprints for a building only after he has created a vision of the structure in his mind. The same is true for executing your will, followed by a broader estate plan. Thought and thoughtful decisions are necessary before the pen touches the paper. There are special concerns if you are married, and the same is true if you have children. The next chapter, therefore, deals with providing for any minor children you leave behind. It addresses not only the care and custody of the individual child, but the management of the minor's assets as well. It guides you through another step in the process that will culminate shortly in the creation of your will.

5

Providing for
Your Children

Put not your trust in money, but put your money in trust.

—Oliver Wendell Holmes

The birth of a child can motivate you to get your affairs in order. You may be concerned about what will happen to your child if the unforeseen happens and you and your spouse both die. I would go so far as to say that if you have children and you are *not* concerned, I'm glad you're reading this chapter.

A new baby is certainly the reason I signed my first will. When I was 6 years old and in first grade, the parents of a classmate died in an airplane crash. No provisions had been made for where Frances would live and who would take care of her. Two factions within the family were fighting over her in court. She clearly wanted to live with one group and not with the other. I recall the afternoon she went to court to tell her preference to the judge. To this day, I have a vivid recollection of her, day after day, crying in the locker room over her situation.

I made the decision at that very young age to never put a child of mine in that heartbreaking predicament. The image of Frances crying in the locker room has never left me. It didn't occur to me at age 6 that money might somehow be involved. I learned long after the fact that it was. Twenty years later, after the birth of my first child, my husband and I were planning a vacation in the Caribbean. I didn't go until I had signed my first will and appointed a guardian for our son in case my husband and I died on the trip.

I had absolutely no property to leave at this point, but my will provided a place to appoint someone to raise our son. As the years passed, we had another child, our family situation changed, and the appointed guardian moved to another state. To keep up with changing circumstances, I appointed different guardians at different times while the children were minors. I always asked the potential guardians if they were willing to take on this large responsibility. As the children grew older, I discussed their preferences with them. Other details may have taken a backseat over the years, but I always kept this part of my will up-to-date.

Ensuring the welfare of your children, particularly minor children, is often the most important estate planning objective for parents of any age. The word "children" has two meanings. The first is "minors," which refers to those children under the age of 18 (14 in Georgia and 19 in Wyoming). This book addresses primarily the parents of minor children. The second refers to "children" of any age—30, 40, 50, and up.

GUARDIANS FOR MINOR CHILDREN

Guardian of the Person

The guardian of the person (aka personal guardian) for a minor child is often the most important reason for a young couple with children to have wills. These parents would want to designate a personal guardian for their minor child to avoid, among other things, the delay and uncertainty that results if a court is forced to make the selection. *The personal guardian will have custody of the minor child.*

Guardian of the Property

The guardian of the property (aka property guardian) manages the minor child's assets. The guardianship of the person of the minor child may be given to one person and the guardianship of the property may be given to another person. As is true with the personal guardian, if you do not appoint a property guardian in your will, the court will appoint a total unknown to handle the job.

THIS CHAPTER PROVIDES FOR TWO GROUPS OF CHILDREN

It provides for the children when (1) both parents are raising the children and they both die a simultaneous death and (2) the parent who is raising the children dies and the other parent is absent due to death, abandonment, or unavailability.

Choosing a Guardian of the Person for a Minor Child (Or, Who Gets Custody?)

If two parents (biological or adoptive) are raising a child and one parent dies, the surviving parent usually assumes sole custody. This is the usual procedure whether the parents are married, divorced, never married, living together, or not living together, as long as the surviving parent is involved with the life of the child. The surviving parent usually gains custody, even if you, the one raising the child, would prefer another person to look after your child.

Thus, all is well and good if only *one* parent dies and the other parent is alive and responsible. *But what happens if both parents die or if a single parent dies and the surviving parent is unwilling, unable, or unavailable to look after the children?*

What Happens if No Parent Is Available?

If no parent is available and you have not named a guardian in your will, the court will appoint someone to raise your child, someone whom you don't know and who has no idea about your values. Not good. Unless you want your child to be in the same netherworld little Frances found herself in, you will appoint a *personal guardian* to care for, raise, guide, advise, shelter, and educate your child, and generally make decisions that are in the best interest of your child—someone who will have custody of your minor child until he reaches, in most states, the majority age of 18.

The appointment of a personal guardian for a minor child is one reason why it is so essential to have a will, regardless of whatever other estate planning you do. Most states allow a personal and alternate personal guardian to be nominated *only in a will*. Other documents don't allow for this appointment. This is your only chance.

The Best Interest of the Child

The surviving parent usually, but not always, gets custody. The court reserves the right to deny custody to the surviving parent or to your designated personal guardian if it finds that such individuals are not *in the best interest of the child,* the standard that all courts use when dealing with children. Generally speaking, however, the judge approves the appointment and considers the surviving parent to be the appropriate choice.

The court would consider a person *not* to be in the best interest of the child only if there are extremely serious and provable reasons. Some of these include alcoholism, drug addiction, serious criminal behavior, mental illness, inability to care for the child, egregious irresponsibility, or any other behavior that is physically, emotionally, or mentally harmful to the child.

Also, the court does not look favorably on awarding guardianship to a surviving parent who has previously abandoned the child, both financially and emotionally, only to reappear after your death to contest your choice of guardian. Abandonment usually means not visiting the child and not providing any support for the child for any extended period, usually a year or so. Abandonment can be declared at a guardianship hearing if the absent parent appears to challenge.

The person you have named guardian does not automatically assume the role. He files a motion with the court asking the judge to appoint him. The court will then decide, based on the above considerations, if the person named is in the best interest of the child.

If You Don't Want the Other Biological Parent to Have Custody of Your Child

You may not want the other biological or adoptive parent to have custody of your child. You may believe it is not in the best interest of your child or you may simply dislike the other parent. Disliking or distrusting the surviving parent is not sufficient grounds for the court to deny custody to a natural parent.

On the other hand, you may believe there are serious and provable reasons why the other parent's supervision would be detrimental to your child, and that the person you are naming is a far better choice. If this is the case, here is what you should do:

1. Name a personal guardian and an alternate personal guardian in your will.
2. Make a statement in your will explaining why you want someone other than the other parent to have custody. There are a number of factors that the courts consider, so answer these questions with the above considerations in mind:

   ➡ Whom do you name as your child's personal guardian?
   ➡ Why do you want to deny custody to the surviving parent? Abandonment? No relationship between adult and child?
   ➡ Why would your proposed guardian be in the better interest of the child? What has he done in the past to support this role? Acted as a parent? Provided love and support? Financial support? Quality of relationship between adult and child? Amount of time spent together? Moral fitness, solid citizen, good role model?
   ➡ Does the child have a preference?

Be sure to tell your choice for guardian that his or her appointment may cause a custody battle. If you foresee a challenge to your choice by the biological parent, see a family lawyer who may give you additional precautions to avert an unpleasant contest.

Please note that a stepparent has no legal rights if he has not legally adopted the child. If you want the stepparent, and *not* the biological parent, to have custody, you must name the stepparent as the personal guardian in your will. You must also make a statement in your will as to why he is your choice. If the biological parent is not available, don't be under the erroneous impression that the stepparent will automatically gain custody. He won't. If you don't designate him in your will, he won't gain custody.

Different Personal Guardians for Different Children

You may name different personal guardians for different children. In this age of children from multiple marriages, it often makes sense to appoint different guardians for the various minor children.

SUPERVISION OF *PROPERTY* LEFT TO YOUR CHILDREN

An adult must be legally responsible for property left to a minor child, one that is under 18 years of age in all states except for Wyoming (19) and Georgia (14). *Therefore, one of the most important parts of your will is providing competent supervision of any property you leave to your minor children, as well as any property minors may inherit from someone else.* You may also have children who are over 18. You may not want to leave property to them outright, believing they are still too inexperienced to handle it. You are permitted by law to impose mature supervision on these still young adults. This chapter will show you how to keep the assets from being released until a child reaches the age of 35.

Tip: If you are thinking of leaving property outright to your spouse with your children as the alternate beneficiaries, remember to name an adult to manage the children's property in the event that you and your spouse die simultaneously.

The planning process involves a number of important decisions. Should assets be given to the children? If so, how much and when? Where should the property be placed and how do you accomplish this? Should a child who is a minor now receive the assets outright at age 18? Should there be some strings attached? How much do you really want to control from the grave?

Leaving money outright to a young adult provides no protection in the event that the child is incapable of properly managing the assets. There is no protection from misuse of the assets, loss of them during a divorce, or access to them from creditors. A safer option is to put them in a custodial device, with oversight. On the other hand, your children may need no protection or you may be averse on general principles to any control from the grave. These are personal decisions that only you can make. There is no right or wrong, but there may be more, rather than less, thoughtful planning.

I will present four different ways you can provide supervision of your children's personal possessions and real estate. Some people decide to use more than one of these methods in their will. A guardian of the property should *always* be named, *in addition to* one or more other methods.

Keep in mind that the property of a minor *must have adult supervision*. The property of a young adult eighteen years of age and older *can have mature supervision*. Whether to impose any restrictions on this latter group is left to your discretion.

The four ways are:

1. Appoint a property guardian to manage the assets of all minor children. (See "Choosing a Guardian of the Property" below on how to do this.)
2. Give property under the Uniform Transfers to Minors Act (UTMA) and appoint a custodian to manage it until the child reaches 18 or 21, depending on the state. Three states allow you to extend the age until 25. (See "The Uniform Transfers to Minors Act (UTMA)" below for a thorough explanation of the UTMA.)
3. Establish a "family trust" to hold property until your youngest child is eighteen. (See "The Family Trust" below for information on the family trust)
4. Establish a "child's trust" to hold property until the child is somewhere between 18 and 35. (See "The Child's Trust" below for advantages and disadvantages of a child's trust.)

Examples of how these methods of supervision are easily incorporated into a will can be found in the appendix.

CHOOSING A GUARDIAN OF THE PROPERTY

What happens if you leave property outright to a minor? As I said before, minor children can only own a very small amount of property outright in most states—usually $2,500 to $5,000, depending on state law. If what you leave is worth more than this amount, there will be a court proceeding to appoint an unknown property guardian to supervise the inheritance. It is far better for your child and for the assets to name someone in your will whom you trust and respect.

One option is to designate a guardian of the property to manage all assets of your minor children that don't automatically come with built-in adult supervision. This can include property that the children receive from others or property you left to your children that is not included in a trust or a custodianship under the Uniform Transfers to Minors Act. *The guardian of the property, like the personal guardian, must be named in a will. It cannot be designated in other estate planning devices.*

The guardian you select must be approved by the court, which has the right to overrule your designation (but rarely does) if appointing that guardian is not in the best interest of the child. It is wise to name an alternate guardian in case the primary guardian is unable, unwilling, or unavailable to serve.

A property guardianship is a somewhat cumbersome and expensive vehicle for management of assets. It requires trips and reports to the court and court authorization for expenditures made on behalf of the minor. In addition to the substantial paperwork, use of the assets is limited and regulated by state law. The guardian must also release the assets to the child at age 18, which some parents consider too young an age to handle the inheritance outright.

For all its drawbacks and regardless of other options you use, it is important to appoint a property guardian for minor children, if only to serve as a backup and catchall to other options. If you want to keep estate planning to a minimum at this time, it is better to appoint *only* a property guardian than to avoid the issue of property for minor children altogether. Your children will fare better, however, if you take the time to include one of the options discussed below. (For more on appointments of guardians of the person and of the property, see chapter 6.)

THE UNIFORM TRANSFERS TO MINORS ACT (UTMA)

Facts About UTMA

One of the most commonly used "trust-type" arrangements is to make a gift to a child under the Uniform Transfers to Minors Act. All of the fifty states, except for Michigan, South Carolina, and Vermont, have adopted the UTMA. Created by a national commission, each state is permitted to make revisions to the otherwise uniform act.

Under this plan, you name a custodian to supervise the assets for your minor's benefit. When the child reaches the age of maturity in your state (the age at which the child is considered to be an adult in financial matters), the assets will belong to the child. A custodianship allows the minor access to funds at a relatively early age. The supervision ends at the age designated by state. In most cases, this is either 18 or 21. Alaska, California, and Nevada allow you to extend the age of control up to age 25. In several states, you can vary the age between 18 and 21. If you feel this is too young for assets to be turned over outright, you may prefer a trust instead.

The UTMA is a good method for small transfers. If the state's age for release of the funds is 18, you can legally use this method for gifts under $25,000. If the age for release is 21 or older, this method is good for gifts up to $50,000, or an otherwise unlimited amount for college expenses.

The following states have adopted the Uniform Transfers to Minors Act:

STATES	AGE GIFT MUST BE RELEASED TO MINOR
Alabama	21
Alaska	18 (can be extended up to age 25)
Arizona	21
Arkansas	21 (can be lowered to age 18)
California	18 (can be extended up to age 25)
Colorado	21
Connecticut	21
Delaware	21
District of Columbia	18
Florida	21
Georgia	21
Hawaii	21
Idaho	21
Illinois	21
Indiana	21
Iowa	21
Kansas	21
Kentucky	18
Maine	18 (can be extended up to age 21)
Maryland	21
Massachusetts	21

Minnesota	21
Mississippi	21
Missouri	21
Montana	21
Nebraska	21
Nevada	18 (can be extended up to age 25)
New Hampshire	21
New Jersey	21 (can be lowered to age 18)
New Mexico	21
New York	21
North Carolina	21 (can be lowered to age 18)
North Dakota	21
Ohio	21
Oklahoma	18
Oregon	21
Pennsylvania	21
Rhode Island	18
South Dakota	18
Tennessee	21
Texas	21
Utah	21
Virginia	18 (can be extended up to age 21)
Washington	21
West Virginia	21
Wisconsin	21
Wyoming	21

Choosing a Custodian

The UTMA allows you to designate a custodian and a successor custodian in your will. It permits you to leave property to a minor by giving the gift to a custodian, who holds title to the property for the benefit of the minor. The custodian has broad powers to manage the assets, similar to those of a trustee. He is given the power to invest, accumulate, and distribute income or principal for the support, education, and benefit of the minor. The custodian is usually entitled to compensation. He is reimbursed for any expenses relating to UTMA matters. You may *not* appoint cocustodians or cosuccessor custodians.

It is usually a good idea to name the person raising your child (the personal guardian) to be the property custodian also, assuming he is competent to manage the assets. The one caring for the child is in the best position to know and satisfy the financial needs and wants of that child. In a situation where an individual with custody is not qualified to manage the property prudently, choose someone with more experience and skill. If it is impossible to have one person serve as custodian of the assets and as personal guardian of the child, then at least choose two people who are compatible enough to work well together for the benefit of your child.

The UTMA permits you to name different custodians for different children. It *does not* allow, however, the custodian to be an institution. The custodian must file an accounting of all funds distributed. He is not hampered, however, by general restrictions from and supervision by the court, nor must he receive permission to distribute assets as the need arises.

Using the UTMA in Your Will

First, mention the specific property and the minor you are leaving it to in your will. Second, appoint the custodian who will have the right, in the words of the UTMA, "to collect, hold, manage, invest, and reinvest" the property, and to spend as much of it "as the custodian considers advisable for the use and benefit of the minor." Third, you must complete a separate UTMA clause in your will for each individual child. Fourth, if you live in a state that allows you to change the age at which a minor receives property, and you want to do so, you must change the age in your will.

Here is an example of how to write a UTMA clause:

Gifts Under the Uniform Transfers to Minors Act

(heading required in will)

"All property left by this will to _____ (minor's name) shall be given to _____ (custodian's name) as custodian for _____ (minor's name) under the Uniform Transfers to Minors Act of _____ (your state). If _____ (custodian's name) cannot serve as custodian, I appoint _____ (successor custodian's name) to serve as custodian."

Repeat, if necessary, for each child.

See personal will clauses and sample wills in the appendix.

Advantages of Using the UTMA

1. It costs nothing to establish.
2. It is easy to establish and to administer.
3. In states that require the property to be turned over at 18:

   ➡ the custodian is free from court supervision; and
   ➡ the UTMA is a good idea only if you are agreeable to the child gaining complete control over the inheritance at the young age of 18.

4. In states that require the property to be turned over at 21 (or up to 25 in Alaska, California, and Nevada):

   ➡ the custodian is free from court supervision; and
   ➡ the UTMA is a wise choice for assets intended for education—a college or even graduate school, since the child has access only after that age.

5. The custodian has broad discretion to use the property as he determines is in the best interest of the child, including but not limited to living expenses, health expenses, and educational expenses.
6. No tax returns are required, but the minor child must file a yearly return based on the money that he actually received.
7. The UTMA is a good method of holding property for more limited sums of money.

Disadvantages of Using the UTMA

The one big disadvantage to the UTMA is that the child gains control of the assets at a relatively young age. Most parents are reluctant to turn over assets to a child at age 18, especially if the assets are worth over $50,000. In fact, most parents tend to use trust agreements that spread the distribution of the property over a number of years, with the children receiving a certain percentage of the trust at ages 25 and 30, and the remainder at age 35.

One can imagine the following scenario. Kate dropped out of school at 15, moved away from home, and adopted a lifestyle that her guardians thought was detrimental to her well-being. When Kate turned 18, the age of legal majority in her state, she faxed the custodian and insisted on receiving the entire balance of her UTMA account. Unfortunately, there was really nothing the custodian could do but go along with her request. The assets were legally hers and she was entitled to them. If the money had been in a trust, the trustee would have retained control beyond Kate's 18th birthday. The money could have been preserved until such time as Kate may have given up her shiftless, drug-induced way of life.

THE FAMILY TRUST

What Is a Trust?

A trust is a legal entity in which one person (the trustee) is the holder of the legal title to property (the trust property) to keep or use for the benefit of another person (the beneficiary). The essential elements of a trust are:

1. the named beneficiary;
2. the trustee (who cannot be the sole beneficiary);
3. the identified property; and
4. the effective delivery of that trust to the trustee.

A trust is one of the most important estate planning tools, and one of the most versatile. Trusts can be created to address many different circumstances. A trust can be revocable or irrevocable, funded or unfunded, established during your lifetime or through your will after your death. Trusts can have varying tax consequences.

Most trusts are used by people with more assets than this book addresses. Tax implications are beyond the scope of this book, for the same reason. If you're interested in a trust other than a family trust, a child's trust, or a living trust, all of which are described in this book, *please see a lawyer.*

Facts About Family Trusts

The family trust (aka the family pot trust), legal in all states and established in your will, allows *all* property left to *all* your children to be made available for *any child's needs,* as the trustee decides. You name one trustee to manage the trust for *all of the children* inclusively. Unlike a child's trust or gifts left under the UTMA, where distinct property is set aside for each child and cannot be used for another child, the trustee of a family trust may spend differing amounts of money on different children.

For example, imagine a family with two children. One is a high school dropout and the other is a serious student with enormous drive and potential. All or most of the money can be spent on the serious student's education. Conversely, if the less motivated child needs an expensive medical procedure, all or most of the assets can be spent on that child.

The family trust, as described in this book, lasts only until the youngest child reaches the age of 18. The trustee is then required by law to divide the remaining assets equally between the children, regardless of how much has been previously spent on each child.

This type of trust can be established for all of your children, regardless of their ages, so long as one of the children is a minor. Or, this trust can be established for only minor children, using a child's trust for young adult children.

Choosing a Trustee

The family trust requires you to name an adult as trustee and another adult as successor trustee. You may *not* name a cotrustee or a cosuccessor trustee. As is true with the UTMA, it is better to name the same person you named as personal guardian. You are allowed to name different trustees for different trusts, although many people opt to use one trustee for all trusts. The trustee is entitled to "reasonable compensation." You may name a financial institution as a trustee, but a human being is usually more satisfactory. Also, it is usually more convenient to name a trustee who lives in proximity geographically, although trustworthiness and skills should supersede location.

The main responsibilities of a trustee is to be honest and to competently handle all management, financial, and accounting duties necessary to properly administer the property of the trust. (For more on trustees, see chapter 6, Choosing a Fiduciary.)

Using the Family Trust in Your Will

First, list all assets you want to include in the trust. Second, complete a separate family trust clause in your will for all children who are beneficiaries of the trust. Third, appoint a trustee and a successor trustee to manage the gifts in the trust. Fourth, you have the opportunity to state, if you so wish, that no bond shall be required of any trustee. A bond is a sum of money often required by the court of trustees, administrators, executors, guardians, and conservators to insure against lost trust property.

Specific Gift Clause

"I leave _____ (list gifts) to _____ (beneficiary) or, if he does not survive me, to _____ (alternate beneficiary)."

Family Trust

"All property I leave by this will to the children listed below in Section A shall be held for them in this family trust.

"A. Trust Beneficiaries
   1.
   2.
   3.

"B. Trustees
"I appoint _____ (name of trustee) to serve as trustee, or if she cannot serve as trustee, I appoint _____ (name of successor trustee) to serve as trustee.
        "No bond shall be required of any trustee."

See personal will clauses and sample wills in the appendix.

Advantages of a Family Trust

1. No supervision by the court is required.
2. One trust can be established for all your children, no matter what age they are, *as long as one of them is a minor.*
3. The property doesn't need to be divided. Therefore, a house or business doesn't need to be sold at an inopportune time,

which might be necessary if you created a separate trust, with specific property, for each individual child.

4. There is no limit to the amount of property you can include in the trust.

Disadvantages of a Family Trust

1. The trustee must turn the trust property over to the beneficiaries when the youngest beneficiary turns 18. If you don't want property released to a child at that young age, the family trust is not for you. A UTMA gift or a child's trust for each child may be a better choice, given the restrictions they can impose.

2. If there is a significant gap between the ages of your children, a family trust may not be the best choice. The older child will have to wait until the younger one turns 18. Let's say you have a 10-year-old son and a 30-year-old son. The 10-year-old must reach 18 before the remaining property can be divided equally. That means that the older son will be 38, older than you may want, before he has access to the property. Given the large age difference between the two children, a UTMA gift or a child's trust may be preferable.

3. A family trust requires more administration and possibly more cost to the trust. The trustee must file a yearly income tax return for the trust, and any trust income retained by the trust over $1,500 is taxed at a higher rate than the child's individual tax rate. In addition, the trustee must do a final accounting when the property is turned over to the children. A trustee is entitled to turn tax and accounting matters over to an accountant or lawyer. In a trust with complicated assets or a great deal of money, there can be considerable work for these professionals, at considerable cost. The trust pays these expenses.

THE CHILD'S TRUST

Facts About a Child's Trust

A child's trust is an excellent depository of assets when you want supervision of assets until the child is older than the 18, 21, or even 25 years of age that the UTMA and pot trusts allow. A child's trust permits you to specify any age between 18 and 35 for the trust to end. It is particularly useful when large amounts of money are involved and you want your child to gain more maturity before he receives the assets outright.

If you believe that a child won't be able to manage money by age 35, perhaps you might consider one of my father's favorite sayings: "Some people mature early, some people mature late, and some people never mature at all." If the latter is the case, see a lawyer about setting up a more sophisticated trust that will last the lifetime of the child and protect the assets throughout this period. A "spendthrift trust" comes to mind.

Choosing a Trustee

The duties of a trustee for a child's trust are the same for a trustee of a family trust. (See "Choosing a Trustee" under "The Family Trust" above and especially chapter 6 on fiduciaries for more information on trustees.)

Using a Child's Trust in Your Will

First, list the property you want to leave to your children, including both minors and young adult children. Second, create the trust by including a clause with the names of each child for whom you want to create a trust. Third, state the age that each child must reach before he receives the property outright. Fourth, name a trustee and a successor trustee. Fifth, state whether a bond is required of the trustee.

Specific Gift Clause

"I leave my ten acres and the house and farm that sit on it in Jackson Hole, Wyoming, including all animals, equipment, machinery, and personal property to my son, Vinnie Mosetis, and to my daughter, Tina Mosetis, or, if either fails to survive me, to the other."

Child's Trust Clause

"All property I leave by this will to the children listed below in Section A shall be held for that child in a separate trust.

"A. Trust Beneficiaries and Age to Be Released

Trust For	Shall End At
Vinnie Mosetis	30
Tina Mosetis	30

"B. Trustees

"I appoint _____ (name of trustee) to serve as trustee of each child's trust, or if he cannot serve as trustee, I appoint _____ (name of successor trustee) to serve as the trustee of each child's trust.

"No bond shall be required of any trustee."

See personal will clauses and sample wills in the appendix.

Advantages of a Child's Trust

1. A child's trust may be the preferred choice if a large amount of money is involved.
2. You may specify the exact age, up to age 35, that a child must reach before he inherits the property outright. Remember, the child receives the property between the ages of 18 and 21 (except for the few states where the age is 25) under the UTMA, and only when the youngest child turns age 18 in a family trust.
3. Like the family trust, the child's trust is legal in all states.
4. No court supervision is required.
5. A separate trust is created for each child.
6. There is no limit to the amount of property that is permitted in the trust if the UTMA is unavailable in your state or if the UTMA age for release is 18 years of age. However, if the UTMA is authorized by your state and the age for release of the property is 21 or older, the assets in the trust must be greater than $50,000.

Disadvantages of a Child's Trust

The child's trust requires considerable administration and possible cost, as does the family trust. The trustee must file a yearly income tax return for the trust, and trust income over $1,500 left in the trust is taxed at a higher rate than a child's individual tax rate. In addition, the trustee must do a final accounting when the property is turned over to the children. A trustee is entitled to turn tax and accounting matters over to an accountant or lawyer. If the trust assets are considerable, so will be the number of hours these professionals work, followed by considerable cost. The trust pays these expenses.

Leaving a Life Insurance Policy to Minors

Life insurance can be one of your estate's most valuable and flexible assets. Life insurance can be used in many ways: as an investment vehicle, to provide funds for your children's education, as a method of avoiding probate, to provide living expenses for your spouse and children in the event of your untimely death, and to meet substantial estate tax costs. Without adequate insurance coverage, real estate, business interests, or other assets may have to be sold at an inopportune time to raise funds to meet estate taxes. Even though estate taxes are well beyond the scope of this book, they are mentioned here as an example of the many ways a life insurance policy can be used.

Using Life Insurance for the Benefit of a Minor

Uniform Transfers to Minors Act

If you live in a state that has adopted the UTMA, you can name a minor child as the beneficiary and a custodian to manage the proceeds from the life insurance. This should *not* be done in your will, but instead by proper forms that you can obtain from your insurance agent.

Living Trust

You can create a living trust and name the trust (actually the trustee) as the beneficiary of the policy. Then name your children as beneficiaries of any life insurance proceeds that are received by the trust. Finally, create a child's trust for those proceeds. (See chapter 13 for a chapter-long discussion of living trusts.)

Managed by the Guardian of the Property

Another alternative is to name minor children *in your will* as beneficiaries of the policy. Any assets these children inherit while they are still minors will then be managed by the person you have appointed as property guardian. This is a viable alternative if your state has *not* adopted the UTMA and you choose not to create a living trust.

How to Leave Retirement Plans for the Benefit of a Minor

It is also possible to leave retirement property to a minor from a pension plan or a 401(k) plan. Follow the instructions in "Using Life Insurance for the Benefit of a Minor" above. You can substitute "pension plan or 401(k) plan" for "life insurance policy"; the same methods and instructions apply. Instead of obtaining forms from the insurance agent, you obtain them from your retirement plan administrator.

When to Use a Lawyer

While my objective is to help you steer clear of lawyers whenever conceivably possible, there *are* situations, I am sorry to say, that require the assistance of an attorney. Consult a lawyer when in any of the following circumstances:

1. You have a child with a mental or physical disability who is going to need ongoing care for life.
2. You want to provide for your spouse but you also want to protect the right of your children from a former marriage to ultimately inherit your property.
3. You are anticipating a custody fight from the other parent or a relative.
4. You want a child's trust to continue beyond the age of 35.
5. You want to place controls over the use of certain real estate property in the trust.
6. You decide it is wiser for a child to receive trust installments rather than one lump sum at a given age. For example, you want the child to receive one-third of the property at age 18, one-third at 25, and the final one-third at 35.
7. You don't want the trustee or the custodian to receive any compensation for their jobs.
8. You want someone to determine how your property will be best spent, at a future time after your death, instead of making that determination now.
9. You want to establish a trust for the benefit of your *grandchildren,* with only the *income* from the trust going directly to your children during their lifetime.

Decisions for and about our children are often the hardest ones a parent has to make. I say this as a parent, not as a lawyer. Yet, that is our job—to make responsible choices on their behalf, until they are old enough to make these choices on their own. This chapter has shown you the importance of appointing a personal guardian to ensure the welfare of your children. It has also described four ways of providing necessary supervision of your minor children's property: (1) You should always appoint a property guardian. In addition to a property guardian, you can hold property under the (2) UTMA, (3) a family trust, or (4) a child's trust until the child reaches majority. Life insurance policies and retirement plans are good vehicles to remember for benefiting a minor.

It is far better to name someone you know and trust to have custody of your children and to manage their assets than to do nothing and allow court-appointed guardians to take control. If you are unsure about whom to appoint, give it careful thought, take the necessary steps, and then trust your instincts. They are usually correct.

6

Choosing a Fiduciary

I want it that mine brother Adolph be my executor and I want it that the judge should please make Adolph put up plenty bond and watch him like hell. Adolph is a good business man but only a dummkopf would trust him with a busted pfennig.

—from the will of Helmut Strauss

Helmut had a pretty good understanding of the role of the executor. He knew the court would watch Adolph "like hell" and that if Adolph did anything unscrupulous, the beneficiaries would be protected since Adolph was required to "put up plenty bond."

One of the purposes of a will is to provide a place to designate a fiduciary. Executors are but one kind of fiduciary. The selection of fiduciaries is probably one of the most difficult, yet important, tasks in constructing an estate plan. There are four different fiduciaries, all with different duties and responsibilities:

1. the executor
2. the trustee
3. the guardian of the property
4. the guardian of the person

WHY ARE THESE INDIVIDUALS CALLED "FIDUCIARIES"?

The word "fiduciary" comes from the Latin word *fides,* which means "trust, faith, veracity, honor, honesty, and confidence." A fiduciary is held to a higher standard of conduct than the average person, with a duty to be honest, diligent, and prudent. The ideal fiduciary is someone who is not only honest, but who also knows your family, and can handle money. Unfortunately, we are all limited in our choices by the people we know, and the ideal is not always possible. Nevertheless, too many of us select a family member without considering whether another person may be better suited.

Fiduciaries carry out the plans you have made. A fiduciary is a person with a duty to act primarily for another's benefit in matters connected with his position, with respect to the trust and confidence involved in it and the scrupulous good faith and candor it requires. The status of being a fiduciary gives rise to certain ethical and legal obligations, including the prohibition against investing the money or property in investments that are speculative or otherwise imprudent. He must not unfairly profit from any financial transaction involving the estate, like buying estate property for less than market value, or otherwise benefiting from his position.

The Executor

The executor settles the estate. His job ends when the estate is settled. The executor's job is to collect and preserve all estate assets; pay all appropriate debts, expenses, and taxes; and distribute the remainder *according to the terms of your will*. The executor has no power to change or withhold gifts or to otherwise exert control over the distribution of assets, disregarding the provisions of the will.

Responsibilities and Powers

Your executor's responsibilities and powers are, in general terms, defined by state law. Most will forms have a standard clause granting the executor all "statutory" powers given by the particular state. Or, they may enumerate specific powers. These powers are generally very broad and flexible, giving the executor authority to enter into all necessary transactions in the settlement of the estate.

These duties can sound overwhelming to the novice. In reality, however, it is usually the probate attorney (if the estate goes through probate) that does the legal work, and whom the executor has the power to hire. The executor's job consists mainly of determining the extent of all assets; locating beneficiaries; remaining accessible to the probate attorney; signing legal papers; paying the funeral expenses, the administration expenses, and state and federal taxes; and making sure that your property goes to the beneficiaries according to the terms of your will.

Choosing an Individual to Be Executor

Someone You Trust

The most important criterion in choosing an executor is that you trust him. Choose someone in whom you have complete confidence. The character of the appointed person is far more important than his legal, or otherwise technical, expertise. This person is often a spouse or other family member. It can be a friend. It can be anyone. It is safe to say that the law recognizes your right to appoint any competent individual you choose, with the exception of any state law restrictions on executors.

A Resident of Your State

Some states require that the executor be a resident of your state. Other states require that an out-of-state executor appoint a resident "agent" in the local state for legal purposes. The probate proceeding will take place in the county in which you resided. Since attending to estate administration will be necessary, common sense dictates that having someone close by will be less costly to the estate and easier for the executor. If the state does not require a resident, and in the event that it is a toss-up between someone nearby who is not too trustworthy or someone out of state with impeccable character, choose the one who is from farther away but whom you trust implicitly.

The following states place residential restrictions on executors:

➡ Florida—A nonresident can be appointed executor only if he is a blood relative.
➡ Illinois—A nonresident *cannot* serve as executor.
➡ Nevada—A nonresident *cannot* serve as executor.
➡ Ohio—A nonresident *cannot* serve as executor.
➡ Tennessee—A nonresident can serve as executor *only if* a resident is named to serve as a coexecutor.

➡ Virginia—A nonresident can serve as executor *only if* a resident is named to serve as a co-executor, with the exception that a nonresident parent, spouse, brother, sister, or child of the deceased may serve as the sole executor.

➡ West Virginia—A nonresident may be required to post a bond.

Beneficiary

It sometimes makes good sense to appoint an executor who is also a beneficiary who stands to gain substantially under the will. This is often a spouse or an adult child. Not only will this beneficiary have a vested interest in how the property is distributed, but it also assures that executor fees will be paid to someone you care about. It keeps the money within the family unit.

Healthy Individual

It is a good idea to select an executor who is healthy, one whom you expect will outlive you. There are no guarantees with anyone's life, but choose someone you anticipate will be available after you die.

Individual's Approval

Before you appoint someone to be the executor of your estate, make sure that he is willing to take the job. Tell him what the job entails. Even though the executor's expenses are reimbursed by the estate, the job requires time and commitment. No one can be forced to take the job. Ask for his approval before you officially sign his name on the document.

Choosing a Bank or Trust As Executor

Most people go to great lengths to find an individual executor, who provides the human touch of compassion. Banks and trust companies can be extremely impersonal. However, there are times a corporate executor might be necessary. Examples of these times are when:

1. no suitable friend or relative can be found; or
2. the nature of the assets may be such that no individual you know would be capable of managing them.

If you can't find an individual to take on the job, then you may want to go to a financial institution as a last resort. It is also better to use a financial institution than to not appoint an executor at all.

Tip: A small or modest estate is usually not of much interest to a large institution, who often will not accept estates of less than $500,000 in value. Small banks may be a more viable route to pursue.

Naming More Than One Executor

Technically, you can name as many executors as you want. Practically, it may cause more conflict than you are aware. If you decide to name more than one executor, you must consider whether each executor can act independently for your estate, or whether all executors must agree in writing before any action can be taken. If all executors must agree, problems can arise. First, there are practical logistics to consider if all executors must sign all papers that the estate generates. Second, what happens if the co-executors don't agree? The estate could be tied up for ages, especially if it must go through the probate process.

You may be considering co-executors to keep an eye on each other, if you don't trust either of them. To solve this problem, you can state in your will that there must be unanimous agreement in writing. This idea is fine if it works, but if it doesn't, there may be serious conflicts of opinion that can only be resolved through a legal proceeding. Think about it. Talk to your family about it, especially the would-be executors. You may find that the better choice is to appoint only one. Or, if you really don't trust any of them, you could name one family member as executor and a financial institution as the co-executor, to provide checks and balances on any decision making.

Naming a Successor Executor

It is an excellent idea to name a successor executor in the event that the original one is unable, for whatever reason, to perform his duties and responsibilities. If you initially named two or more co-executors you must decide whether you want one or the other to serve alone if either cannot serve, or whether you want the successor to serve if only one co-executor is left of the original group. Now is the time to think these scenarios through to their logical conclusions.

Choosing an Executor from Another State

No matter where you sign your will and no matter where your property is located, your will shall be submitted for probate in the county of your domicile at the time of your death, even though you may have died in another county or another state. In addition, *if you own real estate in your name in another state,* another set of probate proceedings will have to be taken out in that "foreign state," but only after your will is first approved and your executor appointed in the state of your domicile. This out-of-state proceeding is called an "ancillary administration" and the person specifically authorized to act in that other state is the "ancillary executor."

Two probate proceedings can be time-consuming and costly, but they can also be avoided with proper planning. There are two simple ways to avoid the double trouble:

1. Place the out-of-state property in joint names, so that upon your death, the property will avoid probate in the foreign state and the surviving beneficiary will receive it directly. (See chapter 2 for information on joint ownership of property.)

2. Place the out-of-state property in a living trust. You can provide for contingencies no matter who dies first, while avoiding double and triple probate and the other disadvantages listed above. (See chapter 13 for a comprehensive discussion of living trusts.)

Investing Estate Assets

After the estate's debts and expenses are paid, but before the estate is settled, does the executor have a legal duty to invest the estate's funds? No, or at least not unless state law or the will instructs him to do so. This is not to say, however, that the executor can ignore existing funds or leave funds "idle." Cash or liquid funds should be placed in an interest-bearing account. If an executor is under no obligation to invest, *he is advised not to do so,* since he can be personally liable for any losses resulting from a bad investment. A "safe" investment is the key here. An executor's first consideration must be the protection of the principal, even if it means a far lower return on the investment.

Executor Fees

Your executor is legally entitled to a fee for services, which will be paid from your estate. The lawyer's fee, if a lawyer is needed, will also be paid from your estate. The set sliding-scale rate varies from state to state, ranging from a fixed percentage of the probate estate (the total value of the property passing through probate) to "reasonable compensation." The sliding-scale rate, based on a percentage of the value of the estate, can be, for example, 5% of the first $100,000 of the estate up to (or down to) 2% of estate assets over $5 million. In a $2 million New York estate, the executor of the estate would be entitled to almost $50,000! The executor should always keep very careful records, in the event that his fees are questioned.

Posting a Bond

A bond is a guarantee that your estate will be reimbursed if the executor mismanages or absconds with your estate property. Many courts require that a bond be posted unless you have stated in your will that one is not required. There is no reason to require a bond of a trustworthy person, since the cost of a bond is paid out of your estate. A bond is normally about 10% of its face amount. This amount will be deducted from your estate and one or more of your beneficiaries will receive less than you anticipated. Certainly, if you don't absolutely trust your executor, it is worth it.

➡ The value of your probate estate is $100,000. A bond worth $100,000 would protect the estate in case of loss or damage. The cost of buying the bond, 10% of $100,000, would cost the estate $10,000. That amount would be deducted from what the beneficiaries inherit under the will.

THE TRUSTEE

The trustee is another fiduciary. The first distinction you must make is the difference between an executor and a trustee. Many people think they are one and the same. This is incorrect; their functions are in fact very different.

The executor settles the estate. His job is finished when the estate is settled, which is usually a year or two after your death. The trustee, on the other hand, manages and distributes the *money and/or property you left in a trust,* which often takes place after the estate is settled. The trustee's job may last for many years after your death, or even after your children and grandchildren's death. Consequently, even when the executor and the trustee are the same person or organization, which is perfectly legal and commonplace, the courts will treat the two positions as entirely separate.

Responsibilities and Powers

A trust is a legal device that can provide a multitude of needs in personal financial planning. There are different types of trusts for varied purposes. *A written trust allows you to transfer the use and enjoyment of property to others, while leaving legal ownership out of their hands. The owner of legal title to the property in the trust is the trustee.* The trust exists exclusively for the benefit of the beneficiaries, with the trustee being responsible for the management of the trust assets. This fiduciary will buy, sell, borrow against, transfer, and distribute the assets to the beneficiaries. The trustee is responsible for carrying out your wishes, as expressed in the trust instrument.

Choosing a Trustee

Someone You Trust Ethically and Financially

As with an executor, the most important criterion in choosing a trustee is that you trust him. Choose someone in whom you have complete confidence, someone who is trustworthy and acts prudently at all times. Naming a reliable trustee is a crucial part of creating an ongoing trust. Naming someone who gladly accepts the responsibilities is another.

Unlike an executor, however, the trustee must also be qualified to handle all management, financial, and accounting duties necessary to properly administer the property of the trust. Sometimes, the trustee's financial responsibility is very simple. For example, the trust may contain only a house. The trustee's job is to maintain it and perhaps sell it. Often, however, it is far more complicated, if the trust includes a large investment portfolio or a business. If the trustee does not feel qualified to handle the task, he may hire financial or investment advisors and pay for their expertise with assets from the trust.

Residency

The trustee is *not* required to be a resident of the state in which the trust is formed or settled. In fact, it is common for trustees to reside and be domiciled in other states or even outside the United States.

Beneficiary

It is more than likely that a beneficiary will also be the trustee, especially the spouse.

Types of Trustees

There are two different types of trustees: individual trustees and corporate trustees.

Individual Trustees

For Oneself

Under general trust law, it is perfectly permissible for you to be the one setting up the trust, the trustee, and the beneficiary of your trust all at the same time, provided there is some other beneficiary (or beneficiaries) after your death. Naming yourself as the initial trustee means that you can maintain full control over your property until your death or incapacity. You can do with the property whatever you choose and have to answer only to yourself.

In the case of one type of trust, a living trust, once the trust is created, you step in as trustee of the trust assets—with the same freedom and power to buy, sell, borrow against, or transfer the trust assets as you had done before creating a living trust. You remain the beneficiary of your assets.

For Someone Else

When either death or incapacity occurs, your trust provides for the *successor trustee* to take over your role as trustee and administer the trust for your own and your family's benefit. No court proceeding or legal action is required. The transfer is automatic. If *you* don't name a successor trustee, the court will do it for you. It is far better to do it yourself, even though you may agonize over the decision.

The successor trustee is not permitted to act for his own benefit or to go against your trust instructions. If any of these things should occur, he will be *personally responsible* for the breach of his fiduciary duty and will be rectifying his mistakes out of his own bank account. The successor trustee has no protection for acting irresponsibly. Not even bankruptcy is an excuse.

If an individual becomes the trustee where *someone else* is the beneficiary, however, everything that trustee does is subject to review and questions by that beneficiary. Investments and distributions and their timing, and leasing, selling, buying, preparing, and filing tax returns and trust accounts must all be done with the best interest of the beneficiary and in accordance with the terms of the will.

➡ A true story: Three adult children were named successor trustees and also beneficiaries of the trust. Each child, according to the terms of the trust, was to receive $50,000 at the time of their parents' death and $50,000 five years later. One of the adult children was involved in a business venture. He cajoled and coerced his two brothers into giving him not only the $50,000 that was rightfully his, but also the other $50,000 that he was not entitled to until five years down the road.

The business venture failed and he lost the whole $100,000. The young man returned to his brothers. He announced that since they were both at fault in violating their fiduciary duties by giving him the additional $50,000 prematurely, he was entitled to receive another $50,000 in five years—to be taken from *his two brothers' shares.* He was correct in chastising them in this manner, and the court gave him the money!

Corporate Trustees

Since people understand the financial expertise and time involved with being a trustee, when it comes to choosing an initial or successor trustee, they often rely on the institutions that have the experience and the time to give the trust the necessary attention and supervision. These institutions are called "corporate trustees."

A corporate trustee is a bank or trust company chartered by the state to accept funds from members of the public under a trust agreement. Although these institutions can be impersonal and not know the beneficiaries involved, *they do know how to manage a trust.* Their fees are regulated by law or by the probate court and these corporations usually let you know how much they will cost before you name them as trustee.

There are two ways to circumvent the impersonal and cold qualities of naming a corporate trustee to manage a trust:

1. You can name your spouse or another family member to be a *cotrustee* with the bank. This will add the sensitivity that can be lacking in a large institution. However, be aware that the same problems with cotrustees exist as with coexecutors.

2. You can give your successor the right to remove the corporate trustee and appoint another successor (corporate or individual) trustee. If the bank is performing poorly or is too difficult to work with, the successor trustee can transfer the trust to one that is more satisfactory. This power could be abused, so consider the individual(s) you have named and use your best judgment.

One last word on corporate trustees. For smaller trusts, let's say $500,000 or less, corporate trustees may feel that the trust is not worth their attention. In such instances, choose a professional such as an attorney or accountant to provide the business expertise of a bank or trust company.

Trustee Fees

A trustee is entitled to a fee or commission for services rendered, but he receives no benefit from the trust, unless he is also a beneficiary of the trust.

Investing Trust Funds

The common standard by which investment decisions made by a trustee are evaluated is the "prudent man" standard. This rule demands that a trustee act in the same manner with trust property that a person of prudence, diligence, and intelligence would act in the management of his own assets, in seeking a reasonable income, and in the preservation of his capital. Prudence is also evaluated by the entire portfolio of the trust and the strategy and investment techniques involved, rather than on isolated individual investments.

THE GUARDIAN OF THE PERSON

As I went over in chapter 5, *every* parent should name a guardian of the person and a successor guardian for their minor children. If both parents die without having legally appointed a guardian for their surviving minor children, the court must appoint the guardian—*without the benefit of knowing your values, beliefs, and preferences*. Courts detest having to do this, because they know the often tragic outcomes.

Even though most states have determined that a child legally becomes an adult at age 18, it is customary to name a guardian until the child reaches the age of 21. As you go through life, you naturally gravitate toward people with the same ideals and goals that you have. These are the people to consider when contemplating the enormous task of deciding who will raise your children if you and your spouse die. These people may be members of your family or close friends.

If your children are old enough to understand that under unforeseen circumstances they might go live with someone else, you can ask them for some input. My parents discussed it with me and between us we selected my best friend's parents. They agreed to the arrangement if my parents should both die. Children normally wonder (and worry) about what would become of them if their parents both died. The process and the resolution gave me security. I would be able to continue at the school I adored, surrounded by the friends I loved.

You might go to a person you would like to appoint and tell him that your children will be provided for financially, and that you hope he will provide for your children morally, spiritually, physically, and educationally. Such an approach is usually agreed to and the one accepting the responsibility is often flattered.

It is also possible, and beneficial, to add instructions in the will regarding the care, education, extracurricular activities, and domicile of the minor children if the guardian should ever have custody of them. You might write, for example, "In the event that my husband and I die leaving minor children, I direct that the guardians make sure the children go into therapy to cope with the loss of their parents. I further direct them to keep my children in the schools they are currently attending. My children are very interested in sports, so I direct that they be given lessons and attend programs that will increase their skills and endurance. I further direct that their religious education should continue. I also direct that loving relationships with their grandparents be encouraged. If at all possible, I would also like them to continue to live in the vicinity of Los Angeles, California." Not only will your guardian be clear on what you want, but the directions will enable the guardian to authorize reasonable expenditures to carry out your wishes. (Chapter 5, Providing for Your Children, offers an in-depth discussion of the guardian of the person and the guardian of the property.)

GUARDIAN OF THE PROPERTY

Here is the legal rule once again: Minors cannot legally own property (including money) outright, free of adult supervision, beyond a minimal amount—between $2,500 and $5,000—depending on the state. Parents of minor children must provide for a guardian to supervise the property that the children now own or will inherit. The will is the standard place to make these arrangements.

If you have minor children who will inherit property, don't forget, or otherwise fail, to nominate a guardian of the children's property. If you *do* fail to provide for this in your will, *the judge will do what you failed to do.* The appointment of a property guardian is a costly and time-consuming legal process. The person eventually named will be restricted and controlled by state law on how the children's money can be spent. The appointed guardian's values may be totally different from yours. Money may be withheld for situations that you might deem essential.

When you write your will, you need to address two different types of property that your minor children may receive:

1. You may wish to leave money and other property to your minor children.
2. Your minor children may receive property from outside sources after your death.

Whether a property guardian is the best way to handle these two categories of property is discussed in chapter 5.

Tip: The best way to leave the property in no. 1 in the list above is not with a guardian but under the Uniform Transfer to Minors Act, in a family pot trust, or in a child's trust. In the case of no. 2, by naming a property guardian in your will, you have ensured that your chosen person will handle all property received by your children outside of your will.

You are now acquainted with the importance of this group of individuals, called fiduciaries, whose job it is to carry out the plans you set forth in your will. Let's stop here and review for a moment. Up to now, you've been laying the groundwork for creating your will. You know what is yours to give away, you have thought about who your beneficiaries likely will be, you have carefully considered how best to provide for your children, and now you've chosen those individuals responsible for settling and administering your estate and further carrying out the terms of your will. It's time now to start on the will itself. I'm ready if you're ready. Just turn the page. Let's go!

PART II

Creating, Revoking, or Changing a Will

7

Making Your Will

I have nothing, I owe a great deal; the rest I give to the poor.

—the will of Rabelais,
fifteenth-century satirist

Most people think of a will first when they think of estate planning. The most commonly asked questions include: What is a will? Do I really need a will? What happens if I don't have one? This chapter will answer these and other questions, including: what a will can accomplish for you, who can make a will, what makes a will legal, who can inherit property under a will, what property cannot be transferred by will, different types of wills, grounds for a will contest, how to prevent a will contest, and what to do with your will after you have signed it.

A will is a simple statement of where you want your property to go when you die. The maker of the will is known as the "testator" if male and the "testatrix" if female. *Everyone should have a will, no matter what other estate planning takes place—even if you think you have nothing of any consequence to leave.* The truth is, *you already have a will,* whether you like it or not. It is not called a will but it accomplishes the same purpose as a will: It disposes of your property at your death.

Let me explain. Every state has laws that will dispose of your estate if you don't make arrangements to dispose of it yourself. These are called the laws of "intestacy" and they divide the estate in the way that conforms to what the average American wants. This is not necessarily what you want, however. If you die intestate (without a will), your state may require your estate to pass one-half to your spouse and one-half to your children. *You* may have wanted your spouse to have everything. No flexibility is allowed.

Even if this division of assets suits you fine, the laws of intestacy do not differentiate between adults and minors. For example, if your children are minors and you die and the other parent is either dead or uninvolved, the court will appoint a guardian unknown to you to raise your children. Another guardian will supervise your minor child's money and property until age 18, the legal age of majority. It seems safe to assume that you would want a say in the people most important in your children's lives. The way to do this is through a will. History shows that appointed guardians are often more interested in collecting their fees than looking after the best interests of your children. (Chapter 5 is very thorough on how to provide for your children.)

Horrifying, also, is the fact that if you die intestate and there are no next of kin as defined by state statute, your property will pass to the government. You will have even lost your chance to provide for close friends or worthy charities or even the care of your pet. Think about it. Everything you have ever worked for—gone forever to the government. You wouldn't want the government to take everything in taxes now. You know you don't want the government to take everything when you die. It is awful to contemplate, yet it happens every day!

Property left by a will must go through probate, which is expensive and time-consuming. I will show you later how to avoid probate. One way is to put your property into a living trust. However, even if you follow the nonprobate path to estate planning, you still need a will to take care of things that nonprobate devices do not cover.

What You Can Accomplish with a Will

There are many things you can accomplish with a will. Some of these things can *only* be accomplished by "executing" (legal term for "creating," "making," or "signing") a will.

Here is a list of things you can accomplish with a will:

➡ Leave your property to the people and organizations of your choosing.

➡ Name one or more alternate beneficiaries for each specific gift, in case the beneficiary predeceases you.

➡ Name a residuary beneficiary and an alternate residuary beneficiary to receive any will property not specifically left to other named beneficiaries or any property that may have been suddenly acquired or inherited but is still in probate.

➡ Name a beneficiary for your interest in joint tenancy property if all joint tenants die simultaneously.

➡ Establish a forty-five-day survivorship period for beneficiaries, including your spouse or mate. This provision requires that a beneficiary must survive you by forty-five days in order to inherit.

➡ Appoint your executor and successor executor.

➡ Appoint co-executors.

➡ Appoint an ancillary executor to handle probate of real estate in another state.

➡ Require or exempt an executor to post bond.

➡ Appoint a guardian of the person and a successor guardian of the person to care for any children under the age of 18, if the other parent is already dead or otherwise unavailable.

➡ Appoint a guardian of the property and a successor guardian of the property to manage the property of any children under the age of 18, if the other parent is already dead or otherwise unavailable.

➡ Appoint different personal guardians or different property guardians for different minor children.

➡ Make gifts to your minor children, grandchildren, or other minors under the Uniform Transfers to Minors Act.

➡ Set up a family trust for your minor children.

➡ Set up a child's trust for any of your children who are minors or young adults.

➡ Name different trustees for different children's trusts.

➡ Change the normal statutory age at which a minor is entitled to receive a gift under the Uniform Transfers to Minors Act, if your state permits it.

➡ Specify assets to be used to pay liens or encumbrances, such as mortgages, so beneficiaries can receive the property (often real estate) free of all obligations.

➡ Provide for what happens if your estate doesn't have enough cash or liquid assets to cover all cash gifts you have left.

➡ Forgive debts.

➡ Specify how your debts and death taxes will be paid.

➡ Include a specific clause providing that if you and your spouse die simultaneously, you will be deemed to have survived him for purposes of your will.

➡ Provide for your pets.

➡ Include a no-contest clause in your will.

NECESSARY FORMALITIES OF A WILL

In most states, a will, to be valid, must follow very strict requirements of signing and witnessing, and in some cases, notarizing as well. *These requirements ARE written in stone. "Almost" complying with the requirements is not good enough.*

Who Can Make a Will?

You can create a legally valid will as long as you meet two criteria:

1. You must be 18 years of age (19 if you live in Wyoming and 14 if you live in Georgia).
2. You must be of "sound mind and memory." The legal test of soundness of mind and memory consists of three elements that must be present at the time the will is signed. This means you must, without prompting:

   ➡ understand the nature and consequences of executing a will;

   ➡ be aware of the nature and extent of the property you are disposing of, at least approximately; and

   ➡ know those who are considered natural objects of your bounty (that is, one's closest family members) and your relationship with them.

Total soundness of mind is not essential for a will to be valid. In fact, the degree of mental acuity required to make a will is *slight,* less than what is required to hold a party to a contract. The law favors allowing people to dispose of their property in the manner they choose—regardless of how unreasonable and unjust it appears to others.

Express Statutory Requirements

The laws of the different states control the validity of the will. You should make your will in the state in which you are domiciled. It's no problem, though, if you move to another state. A will that was valid in the state where it was made will be valid in all states.

What follows is an overview of prescribed statutory elements:

1. *The will must be in writing.* It does not have to follow a particular form or be written in legal fashion. However, it must be typewritten or printed on a computer printer.

2. *The will must have at least one substantive provision.* The most common one leaves some, or all, of your property to whomever you want to leave it.

3. *You must appoint at least one executor.*

4. *The will must be signed at the end by you, as the testator, or in your name by another person acting in your presence and at your direction.* A "signature" is a mark, sign, or stamp placed on the will, with the intent to authenticate the document.

5. *You must sign the will in the presence of two witnesses (three in Vermont), who are NOT beneficiaries under the will.* The requirement that the signatures be placed at the end of the will is designed to guard against fraudulent insertions or additions to an already executed document. Witnesses must be at least 18 years of age and of sound mind.

6. *It is all right for a witness to be an executor, trustee, or other fiduciary of the estate.*

7. *You must date the will.*

8. *The witnesses must watch you sign your name and then must sign their own names and addresses. Like the testator, the witnesses must be competent.* Witness competency generally means that at the time the will is executed, the witnesses must be mature enough and of sufficient mental capacity to understand and appreciate the nature of the act they are witnessing, and be able to testify in court if it becomes necessary.

The appropriate formality of execution is to have the testator and the witnesses in the same room with all involved signing the document, using the same pen, with the testator signing or initialing each page. *After a will has been executed it should never be taken apart once it has been stapled together.* Its validity will likely be questioned.

9. *You must declare at some time during the will-signing ceremony that it is your will that the witnesses are signing.* A single sentence to the witnesses, asked by you, such as, "Will you witness my will?" is sufficient. Or, you can prompt a witness to ask you what you are signing, to which you answer, "My will." Witnesses are not required to read the will.

To get your will admitted to probate, your executor must convince the judge that the will really does belong to you. So that one of the witnesses doesn't need to be found and brought to court to testify, the law provides that the witnesses may sign a "self-proving affidavit." After executing the will, the testator and the witnesses, in the presence of a notary public, should sign an affidavit stating that all of the requisites for the execution have been complied with. These affidavits are generally taken immediately after the execution of the will, before everyone disperses. This done, certain formalities later on required by the courts in the proving of the will can be dispensed with. The executor brings this affidavit to the judge as proof that the will does really belong to you.

Sample will documents and a self-proving affidavit can be found in the appendix.

TYPES OF WILLS

There are various types of wills. I will touch briefly on the main ones.

Handwritten Wills

A handwritten will ("holographic" in legalese) is written, dated, and signed entirely in the handwriting of the testator and *not* executed and witnessed in accordance with the usual statutory requirements. They are recognized in about twenty-five states and even then only in narrow emergency circumstances generally pertaining to:

➡ a member of the armed forces of the United States while in actual military or naval service during a war, declared or undeclared; or

➡ a person who serves with or accompanies an armed force engaged in actual military or naval service during such war or other armed conflict; or

➡ a mariner while at sea.

I *do not recommend* handwritten wills, even in states where they are legal. Judges tend to be suspicious about whether they are forged and the evidence needed to prove that the will was written by the deceased person is often difficult to find.

Oral Wills

Oral wills ("nuncupative" in legalese) are unwritten wills. They are valid in a minority of states, and like the handwritten wills, they are usually only accepted in emergency circumstances such as war or other armed conflict. I also don't recommend oral wills. The same drawbacks to handwritten wills apply to oral wills.

Pour-Over Wills

A pour-over will directs that the property contained in the will be "poured over" to the trustee of a trust. A living trust, for example, can become the intermediary beneficiary of a will. The will property is poured over into the living trust, which subsequently controls who receives the property.

Do *not* use this type of will as a probate-avoiding device, since the *property in any type of will must go through probate*. However, this is a convenient device when used for its intended purpose.

Video or Film Wills

Video or film wills are not valid in any state at the present time. They could be used, however, to show that the person leaving property to others is of sound mind and under no undue influence. If you are afraid that someone might contest your will based on your incompetency, see a lawyer about a video or film will and any other precaution that could forestall the challenger.

Joint Wills

A joint will is a will made by two people, usually a married couple. *When the first spouse dies, the will leaves everything to the surviving spouse and further specifies how the estate will pass on when the second spouse dies—to the children, charities, or whatever.* The disadvantage is that a joint will prevents the surviving spouse from changing his mind regarding what should happen to the property he formerly held with the deceased spouse. If circumstances change—and they usually do in life—the second spouse is prohibited from revising or revoking any part of the will. For example, if you are the surviving spouse and you remarry, that joint property will automatically go to the predetermined beneficiary. Your current spouse will inherit none of that property.

A trusts and estates professor I had in law school said there are two questions that one person should ask of another person before a relationship becomes too intense or committed. These two questions are:

1. Have you had an AIDS test? and
2. Do you have a joint will?

If the answer to the first question is no or the answer to the second question is yes, he strongly advised us to "keep walking" and look further for that special relationship with potential! Enough said about joint wills.

Who Can Inherit Property Under a Will?

Any person, regardless of citizenship, unless shown to be responsible for the death of the testator, may inherit under a will, including one who is "civilly dead" by reason of a sentence of life imprisonment. A gift can also be made to a child still in its mother's womb and is effective provided the child is born alive. Any corporation, domestic or foreign, can receive property under a will. An unincorporated association cannot.

What Property Cannot Be Transferred by Will?

Property that has been transferred into a binding probate avoidance device *can't* be transferred by will. Putting the property in your will will have no effect since for all practical purposes the property has already been spoken for. Once you have placed property in one of the following forms of ownership, it *can't* be transferred by will:

1. Property in a living trust. It goes to the beneficiaries named in the living trust. (Chapter 13 is devoted entirely to living trusts.)
2. Property in other probate avoidance devices, such as pay-on-death designations, and retirement accounts that go to the named beneficiary. (Chapter 12 is devoted exclusively to probate-saving devices, none of which can be transferred by will.)
3. Real estate property that you hold in joint ownership will automatically go to your co-owner. (See chapter 12 on joint ownership of property, which is another way of avoiding probate.)
4. Life insurance proceeds payable to a beneficiary will go to that beneficiary. (For more information on life insurance policies, see chapter 12.)

Grounds for a Will Contest

First, let me assure you that will challenges are rare. *Successful* will challenges are even rarer. You *cannot* contest a will because you received less than you expected or because, in your opinion, the provisions are unfair. You must have *legal grounds*. Any of the following legal grounds, *if proven,* will cause the probate court to reject the will:

1. Lack of capacity—The testator was insane or incompetent at the time the will was signed.
2. Improper execution—There were not enough witnesses or in some other way the will was not properly executed according to state statutory requirements.
3. Undue influence—Someone took advantage of the testator's confused or weakened mental or emotional state and caused

him to leave his property in a different way from what he would
have done if left on his own.

4. Fraud or mistake—Someone induced the testator to sign his
   will as a result of fraud, deceit, or a mistake.
5. Revocation—The testator had previously revoked the will.
6. Bogus will—The will being offered for probate is not the will
   of the deceased. It might be a forgery.

It is very difficult to prove that the testator was not mentally competent or that he was forced to sign the will. The courts presume com-
petence unless shown otherwise. To prove that it was not voluntarily
signed requires evidence of someone exerting a malignant influence.
People who manipulate to this extent are skilled enough to do their in-
fluencing when no witnesses are around.

How to Prevent a Will Contest

A will contest is painful, unpleasant, and expensive, no matter who wins
or loses. There are ways, however, to at least discourage and sometimes
prevent a contest.

There are four ways to prevent a contest:

1. Include a no-contest clause in your will and give the beneficiary
something to lose. Including a no-contest clause in your will does *not*
mean that a contest is legally prohibited. What it *does* mean is that anyone who contests the will and loses automatically forfeits any bequest
made to him under the will. (See the appendix for the actual phrasing
of a no-contest clause.)

You can make the beneficiary lose everything; at the very least, to
make the clause effective, the amount at risk must be enough to make
the beneficiary think twice before agitating in the lawyer's office. Thus,
$1 or $100 is not enough. Of course, it depends on the size of your estate. The amount you decide upon must be sufficient that your contestant will not want to risk his secure share of the estate by attempting to
interfere with the probate of the estate. Many a beneficiary has thought
twice about challenging a will, knowing he stood to lose the sure thing
promised him in the will. Or, to put it another way, the contestant often
determines that "a bird in the hand is worth two in the bush."

Take this example. Bill and Bob are brothers. Their father, Mr. Cook, has an estate of approximately $500,000. Mr. Cook's previous will left one-half of the estate to Bill and the other one-half to Bob. Bill became involved with drugs three years ago and, hard as his family tries to help him, he appears to be uninterested in pursuing a sober life. Bill's father is concerned that if Bill inherits $250,000, the money will only enable him to buy more drugs and continue his present self-destructive lifestyle. Mr. Cook has considered leaving Bill nothing, but he knows that Bill will hassle Bob unmercifully if he disinherits him altogether. Bill has often shown violent outbursts toward Bob. After much thought, and largely to keep Bill away from Bob, Mr. Cook decides to leave Bill $25,000. He also includes a no-contest clause in his will. Mr. Cook is depending on Bill's accepting the $25,000, albeit probably grudgingly, rather than contesting the will with the risk of inheriting nothing.

2. Enter into a written agreement during your lifetime with the beneficiary wherein he agrees not to contest the will. These agreements are rare, with one exception: marital agreements. As discussed in chapter 2, premarital and postmarital agreements and separation agreements usually make clear that neither spouse will contest the will of the other spouse.

3. Put all of your property in a probate-avoiding device. *Probate pertains only to property that is in your will.* (See chapter 11 on probate and why you want to avoid it.) Property passing *outside* your probate estate, such as a living trust and jointly owned property, will not be affected by a will contest. Furthermore, a living trust is not impossible to contest, but it is a lot harder to contest than a will.

If you want added protection against a contest, include a no-contest clause provision in your *trust* as well as your will. The only guaranteed winners of a will contest are the lawyers. It is remarkable how *few* lawyers ever suggest including a no-contest clause. No attorney has ever suggested one to me. However, if you are expecting a contest over an estate, the lesser of the evils is to go to a lawyer now for further precautions and protections.

4. Put all of your property into joint ownership. Joint property passes outside of your will and remains outside the scope of a will contest.

Change of Circumstances

Whenever there is a change of circumstances in your life, you should reread your will and consider making necessary changes. A change in your living situation, marriage, divorce, the birth or death of a child, considerably more or less income or property, a new job or the death of a parent—all of the events that are so much a part of life—necessitate a review of your will and usually a revision of the document.

Divorce

Under the laws of most states, a divorce will automatically cancel the gift to the former spouse. The item will go to the alternate beneficiary or, if an alternate has not been named, to the residuary beneficiary. In some states, however, the former spouse will still inherit. Since the state rules can be complex and changing, just remember one rule: *Make out a new will when the divorce becomes final.*

Tip: As discussed in chapter 2, if you are getting a divorce but have not yet actually received your final decree of divorce signed by a judge, you are still married for will-writing and inheritance purposes.

Where to Keep Your Will

Once your will is prepared and properly signed and witnessed, you must keep the original will and the self-proving affidavit in a safe place. The places that I consider "safe" and therefore recommend include the following:

1. Most law firms have safety vaults for storage of original documents, such as wills and trusts, so this is one possibility and probably the best.

2. The probate courts in most states will, for a small fee, accept your will for safekeeping. It will not be released to anyone but you or your personal representative (guardian or conservator) until your death. The will is placed in a sealed wrapper, along with the self-proving affidavit, in exchange for a written receipt to the person who delivered it.

3. You can place your will in your safe-deposit box. Many states allow a safe-deposit box to be opened after your death for the express purpose of determining whether it contains your original will. If the will

was not filed with the court and it is believed to have been kept in the testator's safe-deposit box, the executor can obtain an order from the surrogate's court requiring the bank to open the box for inventory of its contents in the presence of a designated individual. The only drawbacks of using the safe-deposit box are that questions will be raised of who else has a key, and therefore access to it, and there *can* be quite a lengthy delay in accessing the box.

In other states, however, the safe-deposit box of a person who died is immediately "sealed" under state law until taxing authorities inventory the box. The contents are not instantly accessible to your executor. I recommend that you ask your bank which scenario takes place in your state. On the basis of possible complications in accessing your will in a safe-deposit box, I suggest the safety vault in a law firm or the probate court for safekeeping.

I *do not* suggest that you keep your original will and affidavit in a desk drawer at home. It presents an opportunity for tampering and in the event of a fire it could be destroyed. A *copy* of your will at home, however, is practical. If you feel that the original *must* be in your home or office, purchase a fireproof metal box and place your will and self-proving affidavit inside it.

Congratulations! You have either made out your will or you are well on your way to doing so. People can get quite upset and nervous when they sign a will—especially if it's their first one. A will understandably brings with it the realization that we are not going to live forever. One time when I was about to sign my name, my hand started shaking. I was embarrassed to be so "chicken" in front of the lawyer, but he brushed it off as happening all the time. So, if you feel a bit unsteady, know that you're not alone. And once you've done it, you can give a big sigh, and put the whole thing out of your mind as a done deal!

8

Revoking or Changing Your Will

The law is a sort of hocus-pocus science that smiles in your face while it picks your pocket.

—H. L. Mencken

If you want to change parts of your will or revoke it entirely, you can do so at any time. However, you must do it in a legally prescribed manner that is determined by state law. You must also possess the same mental capacity and freedom from fraud and undue influence that was required to make your will in the first place.

The law takes very seriously the disposing of your property after your death. Therefore, wills must be in writing and signed, and except for holographic (handwritten) wills, which are allowed in only some states, they must be witnessed with very strict formalities according to the laws of the state. Consistent with this approach, changing or revoking a will is of no less importance and must also conform to the law. Otherwise, any changes will not be honored.

To make changes in your will, you can add a signed and witnessed addition, called a codicil, or you can prepare a new signed and witnessed will, with a clause that revokes all prior wills and codicils. Your will can only be revoked entirely by a new signed and witnessed will that contains a clause revoking all prior wills and codicils or through a revocation by operation of law.

Unfortunately, too many people think they can change a will by marking up their original will, writing in changes, initialing or signing their name in the margin, and generally handling changes in various ways that will not hold up under the law. *Never amend your will by scratching out pages or paragraphs and substituting new arrangements and conditions. Doing so will invalidate the entire will.*

Many a testator has tried to revoke his will by writing "revoked," or "void," or "canceled," or words of like import upon the face of the instrument, followed by his signature. Such words are no more valid for revoking a will than are crossed-out paragraphs when attempting to change a will.

IF YOU DECIDE TO CHANGE OR REVOKE YOUR WILL, YOU MUST DO SO IN A LEGALLY PERMITTED MANNER

How to Change Your Will . . .

Add a Signed and Witnessed Addition, Called a Codicil, to the Existing Will

A codicil is an amendment or a supplement to a will, made after the original will has been witnessed and signed. It serves to add, eliminate, or modify some provision(s) of the existing document while keeping the remainder of the existing will.

There are no hard-and-fast rules covering when you should prepare a new will or when a codicil is sufficient. However, I suggest that simple changes in your will—like revoking a clause and then substituting a new clause, or adding a new provision such as a guardian of the property, or changing a beneficiary or an executor, or adding a specific item with a beneficiary to inherit it—can all be accomplished by codicil.

The examples below are some of the simple changes you can make with a codicil.

➡ Inger and Bill have one child named Pup. Until they read *How to Die Without a Lawyer,* Inger and Bill were unaware of the need to appoint a guardian to raise their child and a guardian to supervise the extensive property that Pup will inherit. There is nothing to delete from their previous wills, so Inger and Bill each add the following codicils to their individual wills.

"I add the following provisions to Section 4 of my will:"

Personal Guardian: "If at my death any of my children are minors and a personal guardian is needed, I name Peggy Pressman as the personal guardian, to serve without bond. If this person is unable or un-willing to serve as personal guardian, I name Derek Tessaro as personal guardian, also to serve without bond."

Property Guardian: "If any of my children are minors and a property guardian is needed, I name Giles Anderson as the property guardian, to serve without bond. If this person is unable or unwilling to serve as property guardian, I name Scott Waxman as property guardian, also to serve without bond."

➡ Carolyn originally left an Indonesian wood sculpture to her brother, Humphry. Carolyn now wants to leave it to her friend, Joyce, who has been admiring it and will appreciate it more. Carolyn changes the beneficiary for a specific gift in her will, so she prepares the fol-lowing codicil.

First: "I revoke the provision in Section 5 of my will which provides that I give my Indonesian wood sculpture to my brother, Humphry Jes-sup."

Second: "I add the following provision to Section 5 of my will:
"I give my Indonesian wood sculpture to Joyce Stoltz."

A codicil must be executed with the same formalities prescribed for the making of a will. Thus, it must be typed or printed from a computer, then dated, and signed by two witnesses (three witnesses if in Ver-mont). If you are using a self-proving affidavit, follow the instructions in chapter 7 and attach this notarized document to the completed codicil. You will find a sample codicil in the appendix, along with other estate planning documents.

Here is some additional information about codicils:

➡ You *cannot* revoke an entire will with a codicil. If you want to revoke your will, see "How to Revoke Your Will Entirely" below.

➡ You don't need to use the same witnesses as you did in your regular will, but you *may* do so if you choose to.

➡ Any witnesses to your codicil may *not* be named as any kind of beneficiary in your will.

➡ Your codicil *must* refer to your will. You can do this by la-beling the codicil "First codicil of the will of Luisa Secino [your name], dated December 15, 1999 [the date the will was originally prepared]." The entire will is considered to have been prepared as of the date of the codicil.

➠ If you are making a subsequent codicil, replace "First" with the correct number—for example, "Second" or "Third."

➠ Do *not* insert more than two or three codicils to a will. Too many additions, eliminations, and modifications make for confusion and ambiguities. Instead, prepare a new will.

➠ A revocation of a will by another will expressly revokes all codicils to that first will.

➠ If you want to make major changes to your will, do *not* use a codicil. Instead, make a new will and revoke the old one.

➠ *There are times when a codicil is preferable to a new will.* This is the case when a testator whose competency may be questioned wishes to change his will. The new will could be thrown out on the basis of lack of competency. On the other hand, if a codicil was used, then even if the codicil was declared invalid, the rest of the will could still be admitted to probate and the assets distributed.

➠ Attach the signed and witnessed codicil to the original will with a staple.

Prepare a New Signed and Witnessed Will

It is best to make a new will and revoke the old one if: you marry, divorce, or legally separate; you move from a community property state to a common law state or vice versa; the amount of property in your estate grows or diminishes significantly; or you decide to leave a significant amount of your property to someone else.

It is also advised to prepare a new will when a child is born or when a child dies. If you have an additional child (natural or by adoption) who is not mentioned at all yet not specifically disinherited, that child has a legal right to inherit a portion of your property, as determined by state law. If you have a child who dies, redirect all property left to that child to other beneficiaries. If any of your children die before you do, leaving children of their own (your grandchildren), you should also prepare a new will.

The new will *must* contain a clause revoking any and all prior wills and codicils.

➡ "I revoke all wills and codicils that I have previously made."

or

➡ "I, Sandy Dufield, make this my will, hereby revoking all wills and codicils previously made by me."

When drafting a new will, you *must* satisfy all of the necessary formalities of a will, including the express statutory requirements. A discussion of these formalities is found in chapter 7, Making Your Will.

How to Revoke Your Will Entirely

You are entitled to revoke your will anytime you feel like it. There are, however, only two dependable ways to do this. You can either revoke it in writing or it can be revoked by operation of law.

Revocation in Writing

You can revoke a current will by an express written statement in a new will that contains a clause revoking any and all prior wills and codicils. This new will must satisfy all of the statutory requirements of the previous will, including witnessing.

➡ "I revoke all wills and codicils that I have previously made."

or

➡ "I, Cheryl Clement, make this my will, hereby revoking all wills and codicils previously made by me."

The law frequently provides that a will may be revoked by "an act of burning, tearing, cutting, cancellation, obliteration, or other mutilation or destruction" (or words to that effect) of the document performed personally by the testator with the intent of revoking the will. This can also be done by a person other than the testator, but in the testator's presence and at his direction. Therefore, while you may destroy your will by a physical act, *you should also formally revoke it in writing, by an express written statement in another will that contains a clause revoking any and all prior wills and codicils.* This is the only way to avoid controversy and to make your intent clear.

A will may not be partially revoked by a physical act of destruction. Therefore, the cutting, cancellation, or obliteration of a few clauses in the will with the intent to revoke them, while permitting the remainder of the will to stand, does not revoke these clauses. They remain in effect and can cause enormous confusion.

Revocation by Operation of Law

In common law states, the surviving spouse is entitled to receive a certain percentage of the deceased spouse's estate unless that right has been waived by a written agreement. (See chapter 2 to determine which states are common law states.) In addition, children not mentioned at all in a will may have a statutory right to part of a parent's estate. (See chapter 5 on how to legally disinherit children.)

Thus, the law looks upon the provisions concerning the spouse and the child as revoked if these provisions do not bequeath the surviving spouse the share he is entitled to by law, or if an unmentioned child does not receive hers. All of the other provisions in the will remain the same, although property given to others may have to be sold to collect the money for a spouse or child not adequately provided for.

➡ George and Martha have been married for nearly forty years and live in Florida, a common law state. They have disliked each other for nearly as long, but they have stuck it out for the sake of the children, Rhett and Butler. (Actually, they have stayed together because they're both afraid to go out on their own, but they fool themselves and sometimes others by insisting it has been for the children.) George only likes Rhett and Martha only likes Butler. George decides to draw up a will. He leaves his entire estate to his favorite son, Rhett. He leaves nothing to his wife, Martha, and he never mentions his other son, Butler.

The rule states that in a common law state, the surviving spouse is entitled to receive a certain percentage of the deceased spouse's estate unless that right has been waived by some written agreement, like a premarital agreement. Martha never waived her right to inherit, so she is due her share of George's estate. In addition, children not mentioned *at all* may have a claim on part of a parent's estate. Butler was never mentioned.

The result is that George's will is revoked by operation of law. Martha will inherit under Florida statutory law and Butler can make a claim on the estate. Rhett will likely inherit *something*, but nowhere near what George has directed. To put it another way, George didn't play by the legal rules of wills, so the portions that ignored the state law were simply revoked (thrown out) by the court.

Lost Wills

A will that was in the testator's possession but that cannot be found after his death is presumed to have been destroyed by him with the intent to revoke it. Consequently, the will executed *before* the lost will is offered for probate. In other words, the *last* known will that has been signed and witnessed is the one that is probated. Not everyone may agree that the lost will was destroyed by the testator, bringing ever hopeful beneficiaries to the fore.

If there is no copy of a lost will, it may be probated nonetheless if evidence of its contents and formal signing can be proved. Although only the substance and intent of the contents need to be proved, not the exact words, it is still difficult, since witnesses don't usually read a will when they attest to its signing.

An incident involving Howard Hughes, who died without a will, illustrates some of the problems. Hughes, an eccentric billionaire, died in 1976. Over forty wills surfaced after his death, each claiming to be his last will. As one can imagine, bitter fights began over his hefty estate. The Howard Hughes Medical Institute, a charitable organization founded by Hughes during his lifetime, petitioned the court in 1977 to probate a lost will that the Institute claimed Hughes had signed in 1925. According to the Institute, Hughes left his entire estate to the medical center. According to Hughes's distant relatives, the billions of dollars belonged to them.

Although the Institute presented a rough draft of the will, it was unable to show that the will was ever signed, and it could not produce witnesses to corroborate evidence of its content or its execution. Unable to prove the existence of his lost will, the Institute was forced to accept the court's rejection of its theory. The court decided in 1980 that Hughes left no will.

Hughes's estate has never been settled, but it provides a comfortable income for the army of lawyers who represent the estate and its vast interests in oil wells, television stations, hotels, casinos, real estate, and airlines—$30 million worth of income, to be precise!

The moral? Don't leave your beneficiaries with ambiguities, conflicts, or confusing directions in your will. Adhere to the rules when changing or revoking your will. In addition, place the document in a safe spot, known to your executor, your lawyer, and possibly one other person whom you trust.

You have now finished the section of the book pertaining to wills. What follows will help you plan for health care decision making and financial decision making in the event that you become incompetent and unable to make these decisions for yourself. Planning for incompetency is a crucial part of estate planning. If you do nothing and become incapacitated, the court will appoint someone you've never laid eyes on before to make medical and financial decisions for you. Not good. These appointments will be only the beginning of a legal, emotional, and financial drain on your family members and your estate. It will be much better if you do some planning *now*. There is no time like the present to make these decisions. I've made it understandable and straightforward for you.

PART III

Taking Precautions Against Mental Incapacity

9

Planning for Health Care Decision-Making if You Become Incompetent

There was a time when an apple a day kept the doctor away, but now it's malpractice insurance.

—Dr. Laurence J. Peter

A thorough estate plan must consider the possibility that you may become incompetent and unable to make your own health care decisions. Medical decision making for incompetent people is a relatively new and untested area of law, generally not fully understood by even the most experienced doctor. *Therefore, if you truly want to die without a lawyer at the bedside, you must plan ahead to ensure that your last wishes will be honored.* This chapter will show you how.

For the first time in history, physicians have the know-how and sophisticated technology to sustain your physical life without regard to your acceptable quality of life. If you are dying or in an irreversible condition and cannot communicate, you may wish to refuse treatments that might have been helpful in other situations but can now only prolong the dying process and offer no hope of improvement.

Therefore, there are two things you can do. You can either:

1. do nothing; or
2. complete documents called "advance directives."

If you do nothing and become mentally incapacitated, someone who is unfamiliar with your values, beliefs, and preferences will make the decision to put you on, or not put you on, life-sustaining treatment.

The court, as the last resort, will appoint a conservator (also called a guardian) to make decisions on your behalf. This may occur after family members reach an impasse. Or worse, a doctor may act in ways you would never have sanctioned but that are required of him by law. Medical decision making should be resolved without the expenditure of time and money and without having to involve lawyers and judges in costly and protracted court battles. The patient is always the loser in court proceedings, since the physical and emotional pain of the dying process is prolonged for the time it takes the issue to be decided.

What you *can* do is complete documents called advance directives. "Advance directive" is a general term that refers to any instruction or statement regarding future medical care. Advance directives are used only for making medical decisions, not for decisions about your property or your money, which I will address in the following chapter.

The three basic types of advance directives are living wills, health care proxies, and nonhospital do-not-resuscitate orders.

Living Wills

A living will is a legal document that allows a competent adult to state the kind of care he wants or does not want and under what circumstances, in the event that he becomes incapacitated and unable to communicate. A living will's main purpose is to guide the doctor and "agent" in deciding how aggressively to use medical treatment to postpone death.

Health Care Proxies

A health care proxy is a legal document that allows a competent adult to appoint someone he trusts to make decisions about his medical treatment, including life-sustaining measures, in the event of incapacity. The designated individual is called the agent (also the proxy or surrogate). The agent is given the power to make medical decisions at any time the patient is unable to speak for himself, not only at the end of life. You may also designate an alternate agent.

In essence, the living will details the treatments that the now incompetent patient wants to avoid, while the health care proxy authorizes a designated agent to implement the instructions in the living will.

All directives are grounded in the idea that only the patient has the right to control decisions about his health care.

Nonhospital Do-Not-Resuscitate Orders

Over the last few years, thirty-three states have authorized a nonhospital do-not-resuscitate order, in addition to the regular do-not-resuscitate order that operates *inside* health care facilities. This new document is a boon to the elderly and the terminally ill and must be executed in addition to the living will and health care proxy. It is discussed below.

YOUR LEGAL RIGHTS (OR, KNOWLEDGE IS POWER)

Before I elaborate on these methods of ensuring that your last wishes will be honored, you first need to know your legal rights concerning medical decision making. Most people are so uninformed about living will and health care proxy law that they feel helpless and intimidated when opposed by someone in the medical community. They succumb to pressure to remain silent. The medical community is equally unsure of the law. Thus, inaction prevails and the patient remains hooked up to all that technology has to offer.

As patients, we have more rights than most of us know. It is the competent patient's prerogative to accept or reject any treatment that is recommended by his doctor. Your agent needs to know that he is on sound legal ground when trying to enforce living wills and health care proxies on your behalf. The individual, and subsequently the agent, may need to educate the physician.

You have the right to receive information about your illness and the ways it can be treated. Your doctor must discuss the advantages and disadvantages of each treatment option, telling you the benefits, risks, nature, and purpose of each treatment. You may ask any questions you have about your illness and its treatments. You may want to talk to other physicians in order to get their opinions. You are entitled at any time to find another doctor or even to change hospitals. *The final decision is yours alone.*

You can accept your doctor's recommended treatment or you can refuse it altogether, although the final decision may be a joint one. *Whether your doctor agrees with you or not makes absolutely no difference. Nor does it matter what your reasons are for rejecting life-sustaining treatment.* The physician brings experience and expertise to medical decision making. You bring knowledge of your own personal values, goals, tolerances, and preferences. You can opt for a different treatment or decide you prefer no treatment at all. All these prerogatives transfer to the agent if the patient becomes incompetent. The laws are in place; it is now up to you to become informed, execute the documents, and educate your agent.

ADVANCE DIRECTIVES

Q. Why do I need a living will and a health care proxy?

A. The competent patient is allowed to refuse medical treatment. Unfortunately, it may not always be possible for you to exercise this right. Difficulties arise when you are unconscious or otherwise unable to make medical decisions. You may have had a serious accident or you may suffer from an illness. Two examples of when you would lack the ability to engage in medical decision making are:

1. if you are in an irreversible coma or a persistent vegetative state; or
2. if you are suffering from an irreversible chronic illness such as Alzheimer's disease.

Q. If I lack the ability to engage in medical decision making and have not signed an advance directive, will a family member be able to refuse life-sustaining treatment on my behalf?

A. Don't count on it. Some states technically permit family or surrogate decision making. In theory, if a patient is incapable of making health care decisions and there is *no valid directive,* decisions may be made on the patient's behalf by certain individuals in a given order of priority. In practice, however, if these instructions are not written down, nor an agent appointed, the chances are murky that your wishes will be followed.

Three states, New York, Missouri, and Michigan, allow no one, not even parents or children or siblings, to refuse life-sustaining treatment for incapacitated adult patients unless those patients signed documents leaving "clear and convincing evidence" of when, if ever, they want treatment discontinued. "Clear and convincing evidence" has been determined to be a living will and a health care proxy. Therefore, without advance directives and without decision-making capacity, you will be put on, and you will remain on, life-sustaining treatment(s) indefinitely to postpone death.

Q. What is a life-sustaining treatment?

A. It is a medical procedure that keeps you alive momentarily by replacing or supporting a failing bodily function. The term includes technologically supplied respiration, nutrition, and hydration; kidney machines; and cardiopulmonary resuscitation (CPR), to name a few. When a patient has a curable condition, life-sustaining treatment *is* a lifesaver, used temporarily and then withdrawn when the body recovers. When a person is frail, however, it usually serves merely to prolong a traumatic decline to death.

Q. When will my advance directives go into effect?

A. They become legally valid as soon as you sign them in front of the required witnesses. *However, as long as you are able to make your own decisions about medical care, your advance directives will not be used. They take effect only when you lose the ability to make decisions for yourself.*

Q. Are advance directives used exclusively to refuse medical intervention?

A. No. Living wills and health care proxies can be used equally to insist that physicians provide aggressive treatment, using every sophisticated piece of technology available to delay death. All directives are grounded in the idea that you, and you alone, have the right to control what happens to your body.

Q. Do I need to consult a doctor about my advance directives?

A. You are not legally required to do so. However, there are three reasons why it is highly recommended:

1. you can determine whether you can count on your doctor to respect your wishes;

2. especially if you are currently suffering from an illness, your doctor can discuss the kinds of decisions that may need to be made on your behalf; and

3. the more your doctor understands your wishes, the better he will be able to carry them out. You want to minimize any confusion and uncertainty at a later date.

Q. What can I do to ensure that my doctor will honor my wishes?

A. Choose a doctor who you feel will respect your last wishes. Here are some guidelines to follow:

1. Determine whether the doctor is one with whom you can identify, with an eye toward forming a compassionate relationship. You should be satisfied in your search for a doctor only when you find one who holds similar views to yours, someone on whom, after an honest exchange of outlooks and values, you can count on to respect your wishes.

2. Ask the doctor some questions:

➡ Will the doctor be honest and open even if the prognosis is discouraging?

➡ Has the doctor had experience with the withholding and the withdrawing of life-sustaining treatments from other patients?

➡ Will the doctor comply with your living will and health care proxy?

➡ Will the doctor give maximum pain relief?

➡ Will the doctor deal with an agent and accept the agent's health care decisions?

➡ Are the provisions in your living will and health care proxy clear and unambiguous enough for the doctor?

Q. Do I need to consult a lawyer?

A. No. As a matter of fact, some of the most inaccurate advance directives I have seen were written by lawyers. In addition to inaccuracies, documents from trust and estate lawyers can be befuddling in legalese. I have seen doctors throw them in the wastebasket rather than spend time deciphering them. You need a document that is straightforward, with language and format that is familiar. You are better off with state forms that are available through Gentle Closure, Inc. (for Arizona and New York State forms) or Choice in Dying (for all states), both of whom specialize in advance directives. Information on these two organizations is provided in the appendix.

Q. Am I giving up control when I sign these documents?

A. No, quite the contrary. *You are actually retaining control.* You are preserving your right to make medical decisions through your agent. You choose the spokesperson and you tell him what to say. Without evidence of your wishes, the state decides about prolonging life. If you can't breathe, you will be put on a respirator; if you can't swallow, you will be given food and water through a tube in your stomach, and the list goes on. These treatments can continue for years. Then you *have* lost control and that control has passed to the legal system and the state.

Q. How old must I be to execute these documents?

A. You must be an adult, which is to say that you must be 18 years old (or 14 in Georgia and 19 in Wyoming).

Q. Are advance directives only for older people?

A. No. Nor must you be seriously ill or hospitalized. Tragic accidents, frequently involving an automobile, happen to young people every day.

Q. Are advance directives honored in states other than the one I live in?

A. Yes, although it is a good idea to complete the directives of any state in which you spend consistent and considerable time.

Q. Is there a legal difference between *withholding* and *withdrawing* treatment?

A. No. There is no legal difference between the two. Withdrawing treatment once begun does not expose the doctor to greater risk of a lawsuit. Also, the American Medical Association considers it ethical to discontinue all life-sustaining treatment for patients who are permanently unconscious or dying, if withdrawal is what the patient wants. Virtually all religious groups agree.

Q. Does the Roman Catholic Church oppose withholding or withdrawing life support?

A. No. In his 1995 encyclical letter, the Pope carefully distinguishes euthanasia, which he is against, and the refusal of "aggressive medical treatment," which he favors.

Q. Do advance directives affect my life insurance?

A. No. Withdrawing or withholding medical treatment is not suicide and will not invalidate a life insurance policy. The cause of death is the underlying medical condition that the treatment can do nothing to reverse.

Q. How do I make changes in these documents?

A. You must complete a new signed and witnessed document.

Q. Can I revoke them altogether?

A. Yes. You may:

1. notify your agent and doctor of your revocation in writing; or
2. clearly show your intent to revoke the documents. For example, you could tear them up.

Q. Does it matter if my family disagrees with my wish to avoid a prolonged death?

A. Legally, the answer is no. But the reality is that conflicting opinions within a family make doctors uncomfortable, *even though acting in accordance with the agent's request will not result in liability for the doctor.* It is best to make sure your family knows how strongly you feel. Ask them now to comply with your wishes and to cooperate with your agent.

Open communication is the key to getting your wishes honored and to avoiding legal entanglement. It clears up ambiguities and minimizes later confusion. To this end, openly discuss your wishes with your family, lawyer, friends, religious advisor, and, of course, your agent and alternate agent. The clearer you are on your wishes, values, and philosophy about death and dying, the less chance of influence from family members who might disagree.

Q. How can I ensure that the hospital or nursing home will respect my wishes?

A. Find a health care facility whose philosophy is the same as yours. If possible, request the institution's policy or mission statement regarding the removal of life support *before you enter the facility*. Compare their policy with your philosophy. Make sure they match.

Q. **What can I do if doctors or hospitals are not respecting my wishes?**

A. If your doctor is unwilling to follow your directive, find another one who is understanding and supportive. If you are competent, fire your doctor yourself. Otherwise, your agent can do it on your behalf. Tell your agent what to do. If the hospital is uncooperative, fire the hospital and move to another one. Or, your agent, if you are incompetent, can transfer you to another hospital. In such situations, the original doctor and the original medical facility are *required by law* to be helpful and cooperative in executing the transfer.

It is harder to make these changes than to do it right the first time. So, check out the doctor and the hospital beforehand to ensure that you are all in agreement.

Q. **Do my advance directives need to be witnessed and notarized?**

A. Yes. States differ, but as a general rule, you need to sign your documents in the presence of two adult witnesses and then have them notarized. Also, be aware that:

1. the person designated as agent or alternate agent may not act as witness; and
2. it is far better to refrain from having beneficiaries of your estate act as witnesses. It could cause problems later on.

Q. **Once executed, what should I do with these documents?**

A. These documents will be of *no use to you* if they are treated as confidential papers. Remember, the whole reason for them is to let others know how you feel about certain medical treatments if you become mentally incapacitated. To this end:

1. Keep the original with your important papers *in an accessible place* and *not* in a safe-deposit box that no one can enter except yourself.

2. Provide copies of the documents to family, lawyer, religious advisor, close friends, agent and alternate agent, and anyone else who has an interest in your wishes being carried out.
3. Take several copies with you upon admittance to a hospital or nursing home. Give a copy to the nursing staff as well as to other appropriate individuals you encounter.
4. Give a copy of the documents to your doctor to be placed in your medical records.

Q. When should I make out new documents?
A. You should consider making new documents if:

1. your spouse has been your health care agent and you are getting a divorce (can you envision looking up and seeing your ex-spouse turning off the respirator?);
2. you move to another state;
3. you signed your documents a long time ago (over five years); or
4. your health care agent or alternate agent becomes unwilling, unable, or unavailable to perform his job.

LIVING WILLS

Q. At what point would my physician withhold or withdraw treatment if I have executed a living will?
A. Your attending physician can withhold or withdraw treatment *if you lack the capacity to make your own medical decisions* AND you are:

1. in a terminal condition;
2. permanently unconscious;
3. minimally conscious but have irreversible brain damage and will never regain the ability to make decisions and/or express your wishes; or
4. in a condition such that life-support procedures would be medically futile.

Q. What are some of the treatments I might want to refuse, since they would only prolong the dying process and offer no improvement to the underlying condition?

A. The following are many of the most common forms of life support:

artificial respiration
artificial nutrition and hydration (tube feeding)
cardiopulmonary resuscitation (CPR)
antipsychotic medication
electric shock treatment
antibiotics
psychosurgery
dialysis
transplantation
blood transfusions
abortion
sterilization
chemotherapy and radiation
surgery
treatments to rejuvenate organs

Q. If I currently have a terminal illness, do I need to be more specific about what treatments I wish to avoid?

A. Yes. If you have a condition where the prognosis and the available treatment options are known, you may wish to make advance refusal of specific treatments. Suitable wording should be devised with your doctor and added to your living will. Also, consider including your health care agent in conversations with your physician.

Q. What other personal instructions might I include in my living will?

A. There is a space under "Add Personal Instruction (if any)" in the state forms where you may include other instructions. To give these instruction is exactly the purpose of a living will.

There is a fine line here. If you add too many directives, you may unintentionally restrict your agent's power to act in your best interest. You will want your agent to respond flexibly in unforeseeable medical situations. The following, however, are some suggestions that state the basics yet retain that flexibility. Many of these are included in the documents from Gentle Closure, Inc.

I direct that:

1. I be allowed to die from the underlying conditions or illnesses and to not have my death prolonged through medical intervention;
2. I be given maximum pain relief to keep me comfortable and to alleviate pain and suffering, even if this may shorten my remaining life;
3. I receive maximum pain medication for any pain or discomfort stemming from the withholding or withdrawing of medical procedures including artificial nutrition and hydration;
4. if I should execute a health care proxy, such document shall be construed together with this living will;
5. if there is any doubt as to whether or not life-sustaining treatment is to be administered to me, it is to be resolved in favor of withholding or withdrawing such treatment;
6. I prefer to die at home;
7. I prefer hospice care to nursing home care;
8. my agent knows my wishes concerning artificial nutrition and hydration.

Some states (New York is one) allow your health care agent to withhold or withdraw artificial nutrition and hydration (tube feeding for food and water) *only* if the agent specifically knows that you wish to refuse it. I strongly recommend that you add number 8 to your living will *and* health care proxy. Then, tell your wishes to your agent. Otherwise, you may be placed on or will remain on tube feeding indefinitely. This is a sticky provision in some states and one that must be emphasized to the point of repetition.

9. I do not want intubation.

Intubation is the precursor to artificial respiration and will sometimes be craftily used by hospital staff who do not want to forgo life-sustaining treatment—although the patient has requested no respirator and they know this. If you don't want a respirator, you don't want intubation.

Q. How entitled am I to receive pain medication, especially if I reject life-sustaining treatment?

A. You are always entitled to receive substantial doses of pain medication if it is given with the intent to reduce suffering, even though such medication may hasten death. This is the law (under a 1997 United States Supreme Court ruling) and it has religious approval.

A dying person (or his agent) can reject all life support and focus only on comfort care, frequently called palliative care. Comfort care focuses more on the patient's quality of life and the alleviation of pain than on prolonging life or treating disease. This is the approach of hospice. It emphasizes the relief of physical discomfort with careful attention to the patient's psychological, social, and spiritual needs.

Q. Is physician-assisted suicide available?

A. Physician-assisted suicide is available *only,* at this time, to residents of Oregon. Moreover, it is only lawful in Oregon for a mentally competent individual who is 18 or older and suffering from a terminal illness.

HEALTH CARE PROXIES

Q. What is the purpose of the health care proxy?

A. It provides a place to appoint someone you trust—a health care agent—to make decisions about your medical care, including life-sustaining treatment, if you become unable to make these decisions yourself. Your agent makes decisions on your behalf if you become temporarily incapacitated—after an accident, for example—as well as if you become irreversibly ill or lapse into a coma or a permanent vegetative state. The document also provides a place to appoint an alternate agent, if your agent becomes unwilling or unable to perform. *There can be only one agent and one alternate agent at a time.*

Q. What are the essential elements of a health care proxy?

A. The essential elements are:

1. the name of the competent adult who creates the proxy (you, the principal);
2. the name of the agent;

3. the statement that the principal intends the agent to make health care decisions for him;

4. the principal's signature and the date of the signature;

5. the signature of two witnesses, the date, and a statement by the witnesses that the principal appeared to execute the proxy willingly and free of duress; and

6. the notarization of the document.

Q. Whom should I appoint as agent?

A. Most people appoint a family member or a close friend, but legally, you may appoint anyone who is 18 or older. You should choose a person whom you trust to protect your interests, someone who clearly understands your wishes and is willing to accept the potentially large responsibility of making medical decisions on your behalf, and someone who will not allow his own preferences to interfere if they differ from yours. Also, it is better for you if your agent can stand up for your wishes against opposition from family members or health care providers—someone who is flexible and can interpret your living will in light of the present circumstances *yet able to stand firm against authority.*

Q. Who cannot be an agent?

A. Although this differs by state, you will be safe if you assume that your agent cannot be the following:

1. A doctor, if that person also acts as your attending doctor, unless the doctor is related to you by blood, marriage, or adoption. Any doctor who has been appointed as the patient's agent cannot determine the patient's capacity to make health care decisions.

2. An operator, administrator, or employee of a health care facility in which you are a resident or patient, or to which you have applied for admission, at the time you sign your proxy, unless that person is related to you by blood, marriage, or adoption.

3. Anyone who is already an agent for ten or more people, unless that person is related to you by blood, marriage or adoption.

4. A witness to the living will or health care proxy.

Q. When will the agent start making decisions?

A. Your agent will start making decisions *only* after your attending physician determines that you lack the capacity to make health care decisions for yourself. *As long as you can make and express (even by head or hand movement) your own treatment choices, no one else has the right to make these decisions for you.* "Incapacity" is the trigger that causes the living will and the health care proxy to go into effect.

Q. What happens if the attending physician determines that the patient has regained capacity?

A. The agent's decision-making authority ends and the patient resumes making his own medical decisions.

Q. If a patient lacks capacity and a decision arises about forgoing life support, must a second physician confirm that the patient lacks capacity?

A. Yes. Before an agent can decide to withhold or withdraw life-sustaining treatment in most states, a second physician must confirm the incapacity determination and must enter the determination in the patient's medical chart. If a patient is hospitalized and lack of capacity stems from mental illness, then the second opinion must be that of a state board–certified psychiatrist or neurologist.

Q. If a patient has been found to lack the capacity to make health care decisions, does that mean that he also lacks the capacity to sign a will?

A. No. The fact that he lacks the capacity to make health care decisions is not construed as a finding that the patient lacks the capacity for any other purpose.

Q. What kinds of decisions will the agent make and to whom will they apply?

A. Your agent will make *all* decisions to consent to or refuse any treatment, service, or procedure to diagnose or treat your physical or mental condition, unless there are some decisions you don't want to leave to the agent. There is a space provided on the state form where you can state any decisions that you do *not* want the agent to make. This space is rarely, if ever, used. That is, most agents are granted the power to make *all* medical decisions.

These decisions apply to *all* individuals or facilities licensed, certified, or otherwise permitted by law to provide health care. The term
"health care provider" refers to both individuals and facilities.

Q. How important is it to talk to my agent and my alternate agent
about medical treatment if I am incompetent?

A. It is critically important to discuss these issues. *I repeat, open
communication with those involved is the key to having your wishes
honored and to dying without the need of a lawyer.*

Q. On what basis does the agent make decisions?

A. The agent makes decisions in accordance with your written
and oral wishes, including your religious and moral beliefs. This is why
you want someone you know, rather than the doctor or a court-
ppointed guardian, to make these decisions. If your wishes are not reasonably known and cannot with reasonable efforts be determined from
your advance directives, the agent must decide based on your best interests.

Q. What happens if the agent's directions are not followed?

A. The agent has priority over any other person except the patient.
The agent's decision prevails and must be honored unless the objecting
family member or the health care facility obtains a court order overriding the decision or disqualifying the agent.

Q. On what grounds would one seek a court order overriding the
agent's decision or disqualifying the agent?

A. The grounds for a court challenge include:

1. the health care proxy is fraudulent or invalid;
2. the agent is incompetent or is acting in bad faith; or
3. the agent's decision is inconsistent with the patient's
   wishes, or, if reasonable evidence of the patient's wishes is
   unavailable, with the patient's best interests.

Q. Can my agent be liable for decisions made on my behalf?

A. No. Agents are protected from civil and criminal liability for making health care decisions in good faith.

Q. Do doctors or hospitals run any legal risk by honoring the
agent's decisions?

A. No. They are protected from all liability. There is a growing
trend, however, of doctors *incurring liability for continuing treatment*
against a patient's or agent's wishes.

Q. Will my agent be responsible for any costs involved?

A. No. The agent cannot be held responsible for any cost of your
care simply because he is your agent.

Q. Must my agent live in the same state as I do?

A. No.

Q. How do health care providers react to proxies?

A. They generally react positively. Uncertainty about what to do
makes doctors anxious about a lawsuit. The proxy meets their needs by:

1. clarifying who should decide for an incompetent patient;
2. providing legal guidelines and protection to doctors; and
3. providing a vehicle for doctors and patients to plan for a
   patient's incapacity.

Q. Must health care professionals honor the agent's decision?

A. Yes. They must honor the agent's decision to the same extent
they must honor the patient's decision.

Q. Is there any time when health care professionals or facilities
do not have to honor the agent's wishes?

A. Yes. In most states, health care professionals and facilities are not
required to follow an agent's directive if the decision is contrary to the
provider's religious beliefs or sincerely held moral convictions. The
agent must be promptly informed.

Q. What happens to the patient if the doctor will not comply
with the agent's directive?

A. If the decision is contrary to the doctor's conscience, the doctor
must promptly transfer responsibility for the patient to another doctor
who will honor the agent's decision. The doctor who has asserted this

conscientious objection must fully cooperate with the transfer of his former patient.

Q. What happens if a hospital or nursing home fails to comply?

A. The patient must be transferred promptly to another facility that is reasonably accessible under the circumstances and willing to honor the agent's decision. If such a transfer is impractical or impossible to do, the original facility must usually seek protection under a court order, or it must honor the agent's decision.

NONHOSPITAL DO-NOT-RESUSCITATE ORDERS

Q. What is a nonhospital do-not-resuscitate order?

A. A nonhospital do-not-resuscitate (DNR) order directs emergency medical services personnel, hospital emergency services personnel, or correctional facilities' medical care personnel to not attempt cardiopulmonary resuscitation (CPR) in the event an individual suffers cardiac or respiratory arrest.

More specifically, it provides that CPR will *not* be performed by emergency medical technicians (EMTs) in an attempt to revive you when 911 is dialed and they arrive at your home. Nor will it be performed in the emergency room or if you suffer cardiac or respiratory arrest while in another public place and an ambulance is called.

Q. What is CPR?

A. CPR refers to the medical procedures used to restart a patient's heart and breathing when the patient suffers heart failure and the heart and breathing stop. CPR may involve simple efforts such as mouth-to-mouth resuscitation and external chest compression. Advanced CPR may involve electric shock, insertion of a tube to open the patient's airway, injection of medication into the heart, and, in an extreme case, open-heart massage.

Q. Why would I want to refuse CPR?

A. CPR was created for accident victims who are basically in good health, have strong hearts, and have a good chance of recovery. It was not intended for the elderly or for those who are dying.

When patients are older or terminally ill, CPR may not work, or worse, it may only partially work, leaving the patient brain damaged and in a worse medical state than before the heart stopped. Frail patients often end up in intensive care units following CPR. Under these circumstances, many patients prefer to avoid this aggressive effort at resuscitation.

Before deciding about CPR, speak with your doctor about your overall health and the benefits and burdens of the procedure. Only *you* can decide when enough is enough.

Q. Why would I need a nonhospital DNR order?

A. Until quite recently, a DNR order was valid *only within medical facilities (hospitals or nursing homes), not outside of them*. An emergency medical call to 911 brought emergency medical technicians (EMTs) who, when called to the scene in response to a 911 call, were compelled by law to apply every possible aggressive measure to a patient to keep him alive at all costs. They were legally required to undertake CPR even when all parties agreed it was not viable. They used CPR even if the patient was dead—that is, not breathing.

EMTs have one specific job to do: keep the patient alive long enough to get to the emergency room. Hence, patients and their families were warned that unless they wanted CPR, they should never call 911. Others found this out the hard way. Attending individuals often panic and automatically reach for the phone. Now, however, thirty-three states have given their citizens a new option. The previous DNR, valid only *within* medical facilities, has been expanded to also govern DNR orders *outside* of medical facilities. This means that at home or elsewhere outside the hospital setting (including in the emergency room), emergency medical services personnel will *not* perform CPR on you if the requisite document has been signed by your physician.

The basic imperative, however, remains the same. If there is no evidence of a valid nonhospital DNR order, CPR continues to be automatically administered.

Q. Which states authorize nonhospital DNR orders?

A. The states with statutes authorizing nonhospital DNR orders are: Alaska, Arizona, Arkansas, California, Colorado, Connecticut, Florida, Georgia, Hawaii, Idaho, Illinois, Kansas, Kentucky, Maryland, Michigan, Montana, Nevada, New Hampshire, New Mexico, New York, Ohio, Oklahoma, Pennsylvania, Rhode Island, South Carolina, Tennessee, Texas, Utah, Virginia, Washington State, West Virginia, Wisconsin, and Wyoming.

Q. What happens if I have a DNR order in the hospital or nursing home and I am later transferred to home care?

A. The order issued for you in a hospital or nursing home will *not* apply at home. You must get this special nonhospital DNR order if you continue to reject the use of CPR.

Q. How can I ensure that CPR is not given?

A. All you must do is:

1. obtain a standard, signed form from your doctor;
2. leave a copy of the signed form with your doctor;
3. prominently display this signed form in your home and office plus anywhere else that you spend considerable amounts of time; and
4. check with your doctor about whether your state has a bracelet on which you can refuse nonhospital CPR.

Q. Is a DNR order recommended for everyone?

A. No. If you are in good health and have a good chance of recovery, CPR was created for you. CPR has proven invaluable in the prevention of sudden, unexpected death from an accident or other injury in an otherwise healthy patient. You should probably take advantage of it if you are in good health.

Q. Can't CPR be refused based on a living will or health care proxy?

A. In most states, no. *CPR cannot be refused based on a living will or a health care proxy, because these documents do not usually apply in medical emergencies.*

Q. Is my right to receive other treatment curtailed by a DNR order?

A. No. A DNR order is only about CPR and does *not* relate to any other treatment.

Q. What is the effect, if any, of a DNR order on my life insurance
and health care services?

A. No policy of life insurance can be impaired, modified, or invali-
dated in any manner by the issuance of an order, unless there is something in the policy to the contrary. Furthermore, no person or institution
may forbid or require a nonhospital DNR order for an individual as a
condition for such individual's being insured or for receiving health
care services.

Q. What should I do if I change my mind and *want* CPR?

A. If the EMTs arrive in an emergency, simply tell them to ignore the
form and to administer CPR. Then tell your doctor, in writing. If you
change your mind before a crisis, rip up the document and tell your doctor, family, and friends you have changed your mind.

Q. In a nutshell, what is your advice on how to protect myself
against unwanted treatment, while avoiding lawyers and court
proceedings at the same time?

A. My advice is to plan ahead and plan well.

1. Understand your legal rights and educate your agent and
alternate agent about them.
2. Use good documents.
3. Choose an agent who will be an advocate for your wishes.
4. Choose a doctor and a hospital or nursing home whose
philosophy matches yours.
5. Openly communicate your wishes to those who have an
interest in your health care.
6. Above all, move ahead and execute the living will and the
health care proxy.

These are the most common questions asked about advance directives.
Armed with this information, you are well equipped to understand and
to successfully fill out the documents, which are simple and straightforward and require only a few minutes to complete each form. They are,
however, an important component in thorough estate planning. Since

part of my business in New York was getting people off life-support systems, I know firsthand the importance of having these documents in order. Without them and if the patient is incompetent, your words to doctors fall on deaf ears. It is not the physicians' fault. It is the law.

Sample living will, health care proxy, and nonhospital do-not-resuscitate order documents for New York State, representative of many states, may be found in the appendix.

10

Planning for Financial Decision-Making if You Become Incompetent

The ideal client is the very wealthy man in very great trouble.

—John Sterling

The day may come when you are mentally unable to handle your financial affairs. With any luck, this will not happen. If it does, however, you will need someone with decision-making authority to assume all financial responsibilities for you. There are two ways you can deal with this possibility. You can:

1. do nothing, or
2. sign a durable power of attorney for finances.

DOING NOTHING

If you do not arrange for someone to manage your money and your property and you become incapacitated, a relative will need to go to court and ask a judge to appoint a friend or relative to act on your behalf as your guardian or conservator. A guardianship or a conservatorship proceeding may require, in addition to time spent:

1. a medical determination of incompetency;
2. a lawyer to file papers and appear in court;
3. money wasted; and
4. the appointment of someone you never would have chosen.

DURABLE POWER OF ATTORNEY
FOR FINANCES

A durable power of attorney will provide you with the serenity of knowing that your money and property will be managed by someone you trust, someone who will follow your wishes, without the need for a court-appointed guardian or conservator. This document will eliminate the need for a guardian in the future if you (the principal) execute it while you still have the required competency. You can authorize someone to act in your place, fulfilling your wishes and obligations. The person you appoint is known as the attorney-in-fact. It is a good idea to also appoint an alternate attorney-in-fact.

For example, your attorney-in-fact will have the power, among others to:

1. deposit income checks into bank accounts;
2. make withdrawals to pay your bills;
3. authorize real estate transactions, such as selling your condominium, if necessary;
4. apply for government and pension benefits;
5. handle insurance payments and insurance claims;
6. pay for hospice care or other medical treatment that is not fully covered by Medicare and other health insurance;
7. make tax-free gifts to continue a program you have already started (currently $10,000 per year, per person or organization);
8. undertake any other financial transactions you specify in the document;
9. pay taxes; and
10. apply for loans.

The durable power of attorney document deals ONLY with financial matters. This document has nothing to do with health care decisions or appointing a health care agent to make medical decisions for you. That is done through a living will and a health care proxy, with decision-making authority given to a health care agent. (See chapter 9 for full coverage of preparing for medical decision-making if incapacitated.)

A durable power of attorney may be created by any adult who has "legal capacity"—that is, the ability to understand the nature and significance of what he is doing. The execution of the document itself is fairly simple. The principal must sign the form in the presence of a notary. Although the laws of some states require banks and other financial institutions to accept a standardized form, some institutions will refuse to honor these forms. It is advised, therefore, that you sign both a standardized form and the financial institution's own individual power of attorney form.

Two Kinds of Power of Attorney

There are two different kinds of durable power of attorney directives for your personal property and real estate. They are:

1. Durable power of attorney—The durable power of attorney becomes effective as soon as you sign the document. It states that it remains effective even after you lose capacity to handle your own finances. This provides an effective way to plan for future incompetence as well as for a current situation when you may be out of the country, for example. You can find a form for this kind of power of attorney among other sample estate planning documents in the appendix.
2 "Springing" durable power of attorney—The springing durable power of attorney *takes effect only after you become incompetent* and unable to manage your business affairs. Every estate plan should contain one of these two documents.

Revocation and Termination

Both documents can be revoked or terminated whenever you wish. Although revocation in most states can be oral, a signed statement and notification to all appropriate parties that the power of attorney is no longer in effect is always advisable. The power of attorney naturally terminates when the principal dies.

No Court Supervision

Because most power of attorney statutes contain no monitoring or accounting mechanism, your choice of a trustworthy attorney-in-fact is crucial. Individuals with significant assets or without a trusted relative or friend should consider a trust or other property management device, which will be subject to court supervision mandated by law.

You Need a Lawyer Because a Standard Power of Attorney Is Not Enough

You need to see a lawyer in the following two situations:

1. You want to preserve your assets from the reach of nursing homes or other long-term facilities, or from Medicare.
   Tip: Federal law has recently made it a crime to transfer assets within three years of applying for Medicare.
2. You have no trusted relative or friend to whom you can comfortably give access to your finances with no court supervision.

You have now taken the necessary precautions in the event that you become incompetent and unable to handle your own medical or financial decisions. We all hope this condition never arises, and perhaps it won't, but addressing the possibility saves you and your family a tremendous amount of humiliation, anxiety, time, and legal fees. It is astonishing how a few, simple documents can make such an outstanding difference in a time of crisis.

The remaining chapters in the book deal with probate, why you want to avoid it, and how to avoid it. Included is a chapter on the increasingly popular living trust. You will discover why the living trust has been kept a virtual secret until recently. You will understand why the legal profession has wanted to *keep* it a secret. It's no mystery: Lawyers don't make money off property that avoids probate. A living trust avoids probate. A will does not, and lawyers make megabucks from probating wills. It's as simple as that! Don't allow the probate lawyers to make money off you!

PART IV

Avoiding Probate

11

Probate and Why You Want to Avoid It

Estates should be left to loved ones, not attorneys.

—Walter Heiden

As I said in the introduction, lawyers love large probate estates. Probate, in most instances, is horribly expensive and time-consuming, primarily benefiting the bank accounts of lawyers. A study by the American Association of Retired Persons found the average time in the probate process to be fifteen months and the average cost of probate to consume 5% to 10% of the gross estate. Your gross estate is the total value of your estate prior to any reduction of liabilities such as mortgage, loans, or other debts.

All property passing under a will is probate property. Although wills serve other essential purposes, such as naming guardians for minor children, property passing under a will is subject to the drawbacks of probate.

The bigger the probate estate, the bigger the legal fee. Every dollar you pay your attorney is one dollar less for your intended beneficiaries. Fortunately, there are ways to avoid probate, and, consequently, you can avoid the long, complicated, expensive, bureaucratic nightmare that is inherent in the process.

WHAT IS PROBATE?

Probate is the procedure that each state requires to settle legally the estate of the deceased person and to transfer his probate property—*that is, property that stands in his name alone at the time of death or that would require action on the part of the executor to transfer.* At your death, your debts must be paid, your property must be distributed to your beneficiaries, and any other loose ends must be tidied up.

Needless to say, *you* will be unable to write the checks or sign the documents that transfer the property. The probate court, therefore, takes over those duties with the assistance of guess who? Correct. Well-compensated lawyers. Your job is to circumvent the lawyers by, essentially, *doing their job before you die.*

More specifically, probate is the legal process that includes:

1. filing the deceased person's will with the court and gathering information;
2. publishing notice to creditors and paying off debts, claims, and assets;
3. inventorying the assets;
4. obtaining appraisals for the assets;
5. having the will "proved" valid in the court;
6. preparing accounting of assets and expenditures;
7. filing a petition for distribution and accounting;
8. distributing the remaining assets to the beneficiaries of the will; and
9. closing the file on the estate.

How Long Does Probate Take?

Much longer than you would expect. Most people believe their estate is simple and that it will move rapidly through the probate system. Regardless of how simple your affairs may be, this complex process takes between one and two years to complete. Consequently, the beneficiaries do not inherit any of your property until long after your death.

How Much Does Probate Cost?

A lot. The average cost of probate is over 7% of the gross value of the estate. That means that for an estate of $300,000, the probate costs will be roughly $21,000. This $21,000 is money that could otherwise go to your beneficiaries—in most cases, your family—if you avoided the whole probate process altogether. The executor usually hires a probate attorney to handle all the paperwork and then merely signs where the attorney designates. Generally, 60% of this $21,000 would go to a probate lawyer and 40% to the executor, court costs, appraiser's fees, notice to creditors, and other miscellaneous expenses.

Probate is a windfall for lawyers. State law determines the fees that attorneys and executors can charge. Many states allow attorneys to charge any amount that the court considers "reasonable." In a few states, the fees are limited to a fixed percentage of the gross estate. Moreover, if there are any "extraordinary" services performed, the attorney and the executor can petition the court for additional fees. Sources estimate that probate attorneys, as a group, earn annual fees of *up to $14 billion*.

Tip: Beware of lawyers who try to persuade you to name them as executor. This enables the executor (the lawyer) to appoint themselves as the probate attorney, thereby *collecting two fees*—one as executor, one as probate attorney.

Marilyn Monroe's estate is a stark example of both the amount of time and the money involved in probating an estate. The actress died in debt, but by the time it was settled, the estate had received a considerable amount of income from movie royalties.

1. Time involved:
   Monroe dies in 1962.
   Estate is finally settled in 1980.

2. Money involved:
   Estate total: $1,600,000
   Debts paid: $372,136
   Probate fees: $1,126,635
   Assets available for beneficiaries: $101,229

Is a Probate Lawyer Really Necessary?

Yes and no. One sure way to reduce probate fees is to have your executor appear in court without a probate attorney. A few states prohibit the executor from acting without a lawyer. In states that *do* permit it, there are serious drawbacks to the executor who tries to go it alone: Judges and court clerks tend to be unhelpful, making things difficult for the executor; there are no comprehensive published guidelines of forms and procedures for the nonlawyer to follow; and a mistake can cause further delay and expense, to say nothing of humiliation.

Thus, while handling probate without an attorney is *possible* in some states, it is *not advisable*. It may work, but more than likely it won't. Then you really do have a mess to clean up. It is better to avoid probate altogether, especially for your most expensive assets, keeping your will for any less valuable property and for other important purposes discussed in chapter 7, Making Your Will.

OTHER DISADVANTAGES OF PROBATE

In addition to the expense and the time-consuming aspects of a process that is controlled by the probate laws of your state, there are other disadvantages to consider:

1. All probate proceedings are open in the public, resulting in a loss of privacy. Every detail of your financial life is exposed to anyone who is interested. Your file shows the inventory and appraisal of all your property, the names of your creditors and the amounts owed, plus your beneficiaries and the amount of their inheritance. Confidential business information can be especially damaging if investigated by competitors.

You may remember how tightly Jacqueline Kennedy Onassis guarded her privacy. You may not know that her will was published in *The New York Times* and on the Internet. The list of people exposed to financial scrutiny continues. You can check it out for yourself at www.caprobate.com/wills.html.

2. Probate must be filed in every state where you own real estate. An *independent* probate will be filed in *each state where you own property*. Local attorney's fees and other expenses must be paid before any assets are distributed. If probate is agonizing enough in your resident state alone, think of what it would be like in one or more absentee states or countries as well!

3. Probate is emotionally traumatic for the beneficiaries, who are usually family members and have already suffered the loss of a loved one. The longer the probate period continues, the greater the stress on

the family members and the greater the chance of irreparable family rivalry.

4. Nothing can be sold, as every asset is at a standstill while the probate proceedings drag on toward establishing clear title. Large stock portfolios can shrivel to the point of almost extinction, businesses can languish to worthlessness, houses can be sold at fire sale prices, and liquid assets can be drained away by legal fees. Since the common process lasts up to two years for the average estate, the delay can be very destructive.

Is It Possible to Have Only a Will and at the Same Time Avoid Probate?

The size of an estate determines whether the estate must be probated. Most states exempt small will estates from probate. If your gross estate is less than the amount shown below for your state, you are eligible for an informal probate procedure. Or, a simple affidavit procedure may be substituted for the lengthy and costly regular probate process if your estate falls below the maximum estate value to avoid probate.

Most people have assets that exceed the maximum amount allowed by state law, so few people are eligible for the simpler process. However, if your estate is under the allowed amount, be sure to utilize your state's exemption.

The Maximum Estate Value to Avoid Probate

State	All Assets	Real Estate	Spouse
Alabama	$3,000		
Alaska	$15,000		
Arizona	$30,000	$50,000	
Arkansas	$50,000		
California	$100,000		
Colorado	$27,000		
Connecticut	$20,000		
Delaware	$20,000		
D.C.	$15,000		
Florida	$20,000		
Georgia	$2,500		

State	All Assets	Real Estate	Spouse
Hawaii	$20,000		
Idaho	$25,000		
Illinois	$50,000		
Indiana	$15,000		
Iowa	$15,000		
Kansas	$10,000		
Kentucky	$10,000		
Louisiana	$50,000	no real estate	
Maine	$10,000		
Maryland	$20,000		
Massachusetts	$15,000		
Michigan	$15,000		
Minnesota	$20,000		
Mississippi	$20,000		
Missouri	$40,000		
Montana	$ 7,500		
Nebraska	$10,000		
Nevada	$25,000		
New Hampshire	$10,000		
New Jersey	$ 5,000		
New Mexico	$30,000		$30,000
New York	$10,000		
North Carolina	$10,000		$20,000
North Dakota	$15,000		
Ohio	$35,000		$85,000
Oklahoma	$60,000		
Oregon	$140,000	$90,000	
Pennsylvania	$25,000		
Rhode Island	$10,000		
South Carolina	$10,000		
South Dakota	$10,000		
Tennessee	$10,000		
Texas	$50,000		
Utah	$25,000		
Vermont	$10,000		
Virginia	$10,000		
Washington	$60,000		

State	All Assets	Real Estate	Spouse
West Virginia	$50,000		
Wisconsin	$10,000		
Wyoming	$70,000		

There are pros and cons to the affidavit procedure of small-value estates.

PROS

It requires no action on your part. Just make sure your executor knows that it is available.
The executor can easily handle it so it doesn't require the services of a lawyer.
It costs nothing.
Property can be transferred to the beneficiaries within one to two months.

CONS

The dollar limit restricts the procedure, as defined by state law.

It is not available in all states.

THE POWER AND INFLUENCE OF ESTATE AND PROBATE ATTORNEYS

As mentioned earlier, we are looking at a staggering fee of $14 billion to estate and probate attorneys annually. Is it any wonder that the legal profession wants to maintain the status quo and continue the flow of funds? The only way this economic boon to attorneys will continue is if they keep their clients uniformed, advocating only wills to transfer their assets instead of nonprobate devices.

Unfortunately, some state bar associations are rushing to the aid of their will and probate colleagues to protect their long-standing vested interest in probate, at the expense of their clients. The Iowa Bar Association was the first to declare that any lawyer who works with an organization outside the state of Iowa offering the living trust—one of the most common devices for avoiding probate—will be disbarred.

Other state bar associations have followed. *Other more reform-minded attorneys have suggested that any lawyer who fails to inform a client of probate-avoiding devices should be sued for malpractice.*

In addition, attorneys can create sufficient doubt in your mind about using these probate avoidance methods. If they convince you to use *only a will* to transfer property, they have won the battle. The reason? If you choose either to transfer your property solely by will or you do nothing and die intestate, *you lose.* The lawyers will drain your estate, leaving your inheritors with substantially less than you had anticipated.

I am sorry to report that lawyers frequently offer misleading statements about living trusts in order to preserve power and pocket. Some of the most common statements made by lawyers are:

1. "Your estate is not large enough to justify a living trust."
2. "You don't really need a living trust."
3. "Probate takes much less time than is rumored, especially in this state."
4. "Probate isn't really all that expensive."

These and other misleading statements (to use a forgiving phrase) are simply not true. It's time to let out the legal profession's carefully guarded secret into the public forum.

You Can Avoid Probate

In response to the emotional and financial abuse of the probate process, a number of perfectly legal methods have been developed to avoid probate entirely. These methods, put in place before death, will transfer ownership of property in ways other than by will, thus avoiding probate. To summarize, you can avoid probate along with its abuses by using other documents in place of a will, or by transferring property before your death. The following two chapters will show you how to accomplish this task.

12

Ways to Avoid Probate

Most individuals do not plan to fail; they just fail to plan.

—Henry W. Abts III

This chapter discusses common ways to avoid probate. All of these methods can be accomplished without a lawyer and involve little or no expense. You can mix and match in any way beneficial to you. You may want to use one method for avoiding probate of real estate and another for stocks and bonds. Not all techniques are available in all states and each method has advantages and disadvantages. These differences are discussed below.

Tip: You may not want to go to every length imaginable to avoid probate at all costs for every single item. It is the big-ticket, expensive assets that are the most important to remove from the probate system. After this removal has been accomplished, you may even qualify for the probate-avoiding exemption for small estates. (See chapter 11 for avoiding probate if you have a small estate.)

In response to the drawbacks of probate, and in order to avoid it, many methods have been developed. This means you can use alternate techniques, in addition to a will, for purposes of legally transferring property when you die. *The major probate avoidance vehicles are:*

1. pay-on-death designations, which include bank accounts; stocks, bonds, and mutual finds; government securities; and, in two states, vehicles;
2. pension plans or retirement accounts;
3. life insurance;
4. joint tenancy;
5. gifts during your lifetime;

6. exemptions for small estates; and

7. living trusts.

PAY-ON-DEATH DESIGNATIONS

Pay-on-death designations offer one of the easiest ways to keep money—any amount of it—out of probate. These designations are used for bank accounts (also known as Totten trusts) and government securities, more recently for stocks, bonds, and stock brokerage accounts, and in California and Missouri for transfer-on-death registration for motor vehicles.

The person you name to inherit the money on a pay-on-death (P.O.D.) account has no right to any of the property while you are alive. If you want to use the money—or change your mind about the beneficiary you named—you can spend the money, name a different beneficiary, name no beneficiary at all, or close the account. These accounts remain totally within your control during your lifetime.

Pay-on-Death Bank Accounts

How to Establish a P.O.D. Account

There is a minimum amount of paperwork and no expense involved. The institution—the bank, U.S. Treasury Department, brokerage account, or credit union—will give you one simple form on which you designate the beneficiary. The bank may ask you for the beneficiary's date of birth and address. It's as simple as that. You can add a P.O.D. designation *to any kind of new or already existing account.* The beneficiary, often referred to as a "P.O.D. payee," is not required to sign anything.

Beneficiaries (aka P.O.D. Payee)

1. You can name one or more beneficiaries for a P.O.D. account, except for government securities (U.S. Treasury Department securities—aka Treasury bills or T-Bills), which allow for only one primary owner and one beneficiary. List all beneficiaries on the form provided by the institution. Each beneficiary will receive an equal share of the property unless you direct differently, in which case you can change the proportions.

Tip: In Florida, the beneficiaries *must inherit equal shares*. You can't change the proportions. If you want to leave unequal shares in another state, check your state law or open a separate account for each beneficiary.

2. You *cannot* name an alternate P.O.D. payee. If you designate one payee and he predeceases you, the money will pass to the residuary beneficiary in your will and go through probate. If you designate two beneficiaries and one dies before you, all the money in the account goes to the one remaining beneficiary.

3. You are permitted to name a minor—a child under 18 in most states—as a beneficiary, but be aware of state laws on leaving property to minors. An adult guardian is generally required to hold property until the minor reaches age 18 or 21. (See chapter 5, Providing for Your Children.) You have several options, depending on your state's laws:

- You can leave the money outright to the minor, but the parents will have to go to court and ask the judge to appoint one of them as guardian of the property. As discussed in chapter 5, this is not the optimal choice.
- If you live in Delaware, Michigan, New Jersey, New York, or West Virginia, money left to a minor can be turned over to the child's parents for the benefit of the child until he reaches the age of 18. There is a $5,000 limit in Michigan and a $10,000 limit in New York. In the remaining three states, the amount is unlimited.
- You can name an adult custodian for the property under the Uniform Transfers to Minors Act. The UTMA is valid in all states except Michigan, South Carolina, and Vermont. When the minor reaches the age required or permitted under your state's UTMA, the custodian turns the property over to your child. (See chapter 5 for an explanation of the UTMA.) All you need to do is name the custodian as the P.O.D. payee of the account. On the account form, in the space for the P.O.D. payee, write: "James M. Clement as custodian for Picasso Clement under the New York Uniform Transfers to Minors Act."

➡ If you live in Michigan, South Carolina, or Vermont, none of which has adopted the UTMA, you may still be able to benefit from the law. You can appoint a custodian under the act if any of the following is true: the custodian lives in a state that has adopted the law; the minor beneficiary lives in a state that has adopted the law; or the account, or "custodial property," is located in a state that has adopted the law.

4. Your state law may prohibit you from naming an institution, such as a church, school, or other charity, as the beneficiary of a P.O.D. account. For example, Delaware law requires the beneficiary of such an account to be a "natural person." Check state law if you want to name an institution as the payee.

5. As relationships change, so do beneficiaries. You can always change a P.O.D. designation, but you must follow certain procedures to do so:

➡ To change a P.O.D. designation, you can either withdraw the money from the account or you can go to the institution and change the form previously completed. Fill out a new account registration form that names a different beneficiary or removes the P.O.D. designation altogether. The form must be signed and received by the institution before the change is effective. A telephone call is not effective for making a change.

➡ Do not change a P.O.D. account beneficiary in your will. There is too great a chance that it will cause problems after your death. About half of the states say that a P.O.D. designation cannot be changed in a will. The will provision making the change will have no effect. The beneficiary on the account will inherit, regardless of what the will says. States in which a P.O.D. beneficiary *cannot* be changed by will include:

Alaska	Georgia	Kentucky
Arizona	Hawaii	Louisiana
California	Idaho	Maine
Colorado	Indiana	Maryland
Delaware	Kansas	Nebraska

New Jersey	Oregon	Washington
North Daktoa	Tennessee	West Virginia
Ohio	Utah	Wisconsin
Oklahoma	Virginia	

Some states will allow you to revoke or change a beneficiary in your will if you specifically identify each account and beneficiary. Even so, don't do it. Contradictory will provisions invite lawsuits. Deal directly with the institution instead.

P.O.D. Bank Account Considerations

There are four points to be aware of before opening a pay-on-death bank account.

1. Early withdrawal penalties—The penalty for early withdrawal is usually waived if you die before that term expires and your beneficiary claims the assets.

2. Your spouse's rights—Your spouse may have rights to your P.O.D. account, even though the assets are in your name. If you live in a common law state, your spouse is entitled to a certain percentage of your property at death. This amount is called the spouse's "statutory share." The funds in a P.O.D. account may be subject to a spouse's claim, depending on the dollar amount of the other assets you have left. If you live in a community property state, your spouse probably already owns one-half of whatever is in the account, even if the account is in your name only. (See chapter 2, Property Rules for Married Couples.)

3. Creditors' claims—A P.O.D. account may be subject to the claims of creditors, if there are not enough assets to either pay your debts or pay for any probate procedures that might occur.

4. State death taxes—If your state has a state death tax, death tax liens may be imposed on your accounts. Liens must be paid and removed before assets may be transferred to the beneficiary.

Claiming the Money from a P.O.D. Bank Account

To claim the money after your death, the P.O.D. beneficiary need only show the bank a certified copy of your death certificate and proof of the beneficiary's identity. The bank will then release the money, since it is not under the control of the probate court. The money automatically belongs to the beneficiary when you die. Practically speaking, there may be delays when the money is claimed. Vermont, for example, doesn't allow the bank to release the money until ninety days after the death of the account owner. But such delays are minimal compared to probate delays.

Government Securities

You can also name someone to inherit certain kinds of government securities, including Treasury bills and notes and savings bonds. You can hold these securities in a pay-on-death "beneficiary" form. In a form that either your investment advisor or the Treasury Department can provide, you register ownership of your securities in your name, followed by "payable on death to" and the name of the beneficiary. For Internet information about savings bonds, Treasury bills, notes, and bonds, check out www.publicdebt.treas.gov.

The transfer-on-death beneficiary for government securities *must be a person, not an organization.* As previously mentioned, there can be only one primary owner and one beneficiary. These securities also pass outside of probate, although federal and state death taxes must be paid on them, if your estate is larger than the exempted amount. (See chapter 3, Inventory Your Property.) You can name a different beneficiary at any time by filling out new ownership documents. You have complete control over these assets.

Brokerage Accounts, Stock and Bonds, and Mutual Funds

In a majority of states, you can add a transfer-on-death designation to brokerage accounts, individual securities (stocks and bonds), and mutual funds by signing a form naming a beneficiary for each account as supplied by your broker. The law doesn't *require* stockbrokers and corporate transfer agents to offer transfer-on-death registration in the states that permit it. It merely makes this option possible. These transfer-on-death registration of securities are provided for under the Uniform Transfers-on-Death Securities Registration Act and are allowed in the following states:

Alabama	Maryland	Oklahoma
Alaska	Minnesota	Oregon
Arizona	Mississippi	Pennsylvania
Arkansas	Missouri	South Dakota
Colorado	Montana	Tennessee
Connecticut	Nebraska	Texas
Delaware	Nevada	Utah
Florida	New Hampshire	Virginia
Idaho	New Jersey	Washington
Illinois	New Mexico	West Virginia
Iowa	North Dakota	Wisconsin
Kansas	Ohio	Wyoming

Even if you don't live in one of these states, it may still be possible to use transfer-on-death designation for securities if any of the following apply:

➡ The issuer of the stock or the stockbroker is incorporated in a state that has adopted the law.
➡ The stockbroker's principal office is in a state that has adopted the law.
➡ The office making the registration is in a state that has adopted the law.
➡ The transfer agent's office is located in a state that has adopted the law.

You are always free to change the transfer-on-death beneficiary of your securities. For the change to take effect, contact the broker or transfer agent and redo the ownership document itself. The beneficiary can easily claim the assets after your death by showing the transfer agent or broker a certified copy of the death certificate and proof of his identity.

Vehicles

Only two states, California and Missouri, allow car owners the option of naming a beneficiary, right on the registration form, to inherit the vehicle. I hope the practice will spread. It is a simple and free way for people to pass on their cars, trucks, and even small boats. All you need do is apply at the local Department of Motor Vehicles for a certificate of car ownership in "beneficiary form."

The beneficiary will automatically own the vehicle after your death, although he has no rights to it as long as you are alive. You remain free to sell or give away the car at any time, and to name someone else as the beneficiary. To revoke or change a beneficiary, you can either sell or give away the vehicle, or you can apply for a new certificate of ownership, one that names another beneficiary or no beneficiary at all.

Under Missouri law, the car owner can designate on the vehicle's title document *one or more beneficiaries* to receive ownership of the car upon your death. The California law allows for the car owner to designate *only one beneficiary*. These transfers are done without court proceedings.

Since these laws are somewhat new, particularly in California, it may prove helpful to know that this probate avoidance device is Section 4150.7 of the Vehicle Code. In California, transfer-on-death registration is also available for certain boats, called "undocumented vessels," which include small boats that aren't required to have a valid marine document from the U.S. Bureau of Customs. Only one owner and one beneficiary may be listed. This device is Section 9852.7 of the California Vehicle Code. This beneficiary form of registration for vehicles and small boats is a simple way to avoid probate. Other states would be well served by adopting similar laws of transfer.

RETIREMENT ACCOUNTS

Millions of people are now in charge of one or more retirement programs, such as Social Security payments, military benefits, public or private employee pensions, union pension plans, or individual retirement programs. Another method of avoiding probate involves naming a beneficiary to these retirement accounts. More than half a trillion dollars has been invested to date in 401(k) plans alone.

These retirement plans are excellent estate planning devices in that their transfer after death does not involve probate entanglement. They can also be advantageous from a tax standpoint. This section will consider three retirement benefits—Social Security, individual retirement programs, and pensions—and their transfer upon the worker's death.

Social Security

Social Security reflects a national commitment to providing a public pension to older workers. Most elderly Americans and their spouses are covered by this program. Social Security payments are adjusted to represent the changing costs of living, contributing to the economic security of older Americans. Payment usually begins at age 65, although it is possible to receive reduced payments at age 55, or even younger if you are blind or disabled. Payments to people *under age 70* may be reduced if earnings are above a designated amount. There are no such reductions over age 70, regardless of the amount.

Social Security also provides payments to many surviving relatives of the worker, regardless of their own earning record. The government gives benefits to prescribed people at determined amounts. It provides one lump sum of $255 at the time of death to the surviving spouse or child eligible for benefits. The following people are usually entitled to receive benefits based on the deceased wage earner's income:

Surviving Spouse
A surviving spouse who is 65 or older receives, for life, 100% of the deceased spouse's Social Security benefits if the deceased spouse was over age 65 at the time of death. A surviving spouse between age 60 and 65 receives a smaller amount.

Former Spouse
If the marriage lasted ten years or longer, the former spouse of the deceased person, who has not remarried by age 60, receives payment for life: full benefits at age 65, and reduced benefits starting from age 60.

Unmarried Children
Children up to age 18 (19 if attending high school full time) receive payments.

Children Disabled Before Age 22

Children disabled before age 22 can get benefits for as long as they are disabled.

Individual Retirement Programs

Many millions of people contribute to one or more individual retirement programs to provide them with assets when they retire. Money in an individual retirement program, such as an IRA, a Roth IRA, or a 401(k) account, that is left to a named beneficiary at the deceased owner's death does not go through probate. The administrator of the plan pays the funds directly to the named beneficiary. Consider these accounts when you contemplate estate planning with an eye toward avoiding probate.

Common Retirement Programs

Traditional IRAs and 401(k) Plans

- The money you deposit each year is tax deductible.
- The amount you are legally allowed to deposit depends on your type of retirement plan.
- The income you deposit and the profits you earn from invested money are not taxed now.
- At some point in time, you must begin making withdrawals.
- Withdrawals are subject to an income tax.
- The account passes to the beneficiary *without probate*.

Roth IRAs

- The money you deposit is *not* tax deductible.
- The income accumulates tax-free as long as it stays in the account at least five years.
- At no time are you forced to make withdrawals.
- Withdrawals are *not* subject to an income tax.
- The account passes to the beneficiary *without probate*.

The Roth is one of the biggest single investment tax breaks Congress has ever given to middle-class Americans—especially those who are diligent savers. A big difference between a Roth IRA and a regular IRA involves the timing of tax payments. A Roth is built with money you have left after you pay the government, but it allows you to withdraw money tax free at retirement. By paying up front, you are essentially betting that tax rates won't fall in the future, or that you won't be in a lower tax bracket when it comes time to withdraw money from your account. In traditional IRAs and 401(k) plans, the income you deposit and the profits you earn from invested money are not taxed now. Taxation occurs when the money is later taken out of the account.

Beneficiaries of Your Retirement Programs

You can always name a beneficiary for an individual retirement program. If you are single, you can name anyone you choose as beneficiary. If you are married, however, the law may place restrictions on your choices. When you open one of these accounts—an IRA, a Roth IRA, or a 401(k) account—you will fill out a form that asks you to name a beneficiary. You will probably be given the opportunity to also name an alternate beneficiary, who will inherit the proceeds if the primary beneficiary predeceases you.

Restrictions if You Are Married

401(k) Accounts
Your spouse is entitled to inherit all of the money in your 401(k) account, unless he signs a written waiver consenting to your choice of another beneficiary. The waiver is provided by the firm that administers the plan, and a plan representative or notary public must be a witness to the writing. A prenuptial plan does not cover a waiver, which must be executed separately.

IRAs
If you live in a common law state, you are able to name anyone you choose as your beneficiary. However, if you live in a community property state (Arizona, California, Idaho, Louisiana, Nevada, New Mexico, Texas, Washington, or Wisconsin), the chances are good that your spouse already owns one-half of the retirement account. If you earned

the money during your marriage, the money is community property and your spouse automatically owns one-half. As a general rule, therefore, if you want to name someone other than your spouse in a community property state, get your spouse's consent in writing. (See chapter 2 for a discussion of community property.)

Naming an Adult Other Than Your Spouse As Beneficiary

If you name two or more individuals as beneficiaries, they will get equal shares unless you specify otherwise.

If you die BEFORE age 70 ½, the beneficiary can either withdraw all the money within five years of your death or withdraw the money over his own life expectancy, postponing the income tax that is due. Not all plans allow the latter distribution.

If you die AFTER age 70 ½, your beneficiary's minimum withdrawal will be the same as yours would have been, had you lived. For a Roth IRA, the beneficiary has the same options as if you had died before age 70½—due to the fact that no mandatory lifetime withdrawals exist.

Naming Minor Children As Beneficiaries

Minor children are often named as the beneficiaries of retirement accounts. Keep in mind, however, that if a minor inherits more than a few thousand dollars, the parents must go to court and have a guardian of the property appointed. The easiest way around this, if your state law allows it, is to name a custodian in your will under the Uniform Transfer to Minors Act.

Tip: Be aware, also, that the beneficiary of a retirement program (except funds in a Roth IRA) will have to pay income tax on any money received.

Naming Your Estate As Beneficiary

It is not a good idea to name your estate as the beneficiary of your retirement plan, since doing so will ensure that the money in the account will go through probate. One of the benefits of retirement plans is that they avoid probate. The estate is the only beneficiary that requires probate before distribution.

Naming a Living Trust As Beneficiary

There is no advantage in doing this and the tax consequences could be unfavorable. It is better to leave the account directly to the beneficiary. (See chapter 13 for a full explanation of living trusts.)

Pensions

There are many types of pension programs. You have no control over how the money is invested, and it's at your employer's discretion whether you have a pension plan at all. Your company or organization that sets up a pension plan determines how and when you will receive the benefits. There is also no legal requirement that a pension plan pay death benefits—to your spouse or anyone else. Some employers are generous and some are stingy.

Your right to receive payments may or may not extend to your surviving spouse or other beneficiaries. If you have a vested right in a pension (and such is not always the case), you may name a beneficiary to inherit your vested rights. Your plan administrator is required to give you a statement of how much your plan would pay to a surviving spouse or other beneficiary when you die. Money that goes to a beneficiary under a pension plan is not subject to probate.

LIFE INSURANCE

Life insurance has long been a part of estate planning in the United States. In fact, Americans currently hold an estimated two trillion dollars worth of life insurance, far more, per capita, than any other nationality. Life insurance single-handedly satisfies multiple estate planning objectives simultaneously. As such, adequate coverage is one of the crucial components of a successful estate plan. In many estates, life insurance may be the largest single asset. The ability to remove the taxable aspect of property out of an estate is one of the most effective planning strategies. Life insurance, unlike any other asset, develops its optimum value at the time of death.

For our purposes especially, life insurance proceeds avoid probate because you name your beneficiary in the policy instead of in your will. This means that the proceeds can be transferred quickly to survivors with little red tape, cost, or delay.

Why You Need Life Insurance

There are various reasons why you may want to acquire life insurance, including:

1. the replacement of lost income by the death of a wage earner;
2. the proceeds provide immediate cash at death, a handy source of cash to pay the deceased's debts, funeral expenses, and income or death taxes;
3. the proceeds provide liquidity for an estate and thereby prevent the forced sale of assets to satisfy estate taxes;
4. the proceeds avoid probate, transferring assets quickly without cost or delay; and
5. life insurance can significantly reduce death tax liability of the insurer's estate when a policy is not legally owned by the person who is the insured. The insurance proceeds are subsequently removed from the estate. This is a benefit, of course, only if your estate is large enough to be forced to deal with death tax liability in the first place.

A Word of Caution Before Buying Insurance

There is no national or federal insurance guarantee fund for life insurance companies similar to FDIC insurance for bank depositors. To avoid serious disappointment, check the reliability of the insurance company you plan to use. Several companies rate the financial stability of insurance companies. *Check your insurance company against one of these rating systems.* You should be able to locate the following reports by checking your local library and accessing the Internet. The names of two major rating companies are:

➡ Moody's Investors Service
➡ Standard & Poor's

Types of Life Insurance

For estate planning purposes, there are two main types of life insurance: term insurance, which provides insurance only for a set period;

and "permanent" insurance, which the company can never cancel as long as the premiums are paid.

Life Insurance and Probate

The proceeds of a life insurance policy are not subject to probate unless you name your estate as the beneficiary of your policy. If anyone else, including a trust, is the beneficiary of the policy, the proceeds are not included in the probate estate, but are instead paid to the beneficiary directly without the cost and delay of probate.

Choosing Life Insurance Beneficiaries

When you buy life insurance, you name the policy's beneficiaries. You can change these beneficiaries at any time as long as you are mentally competent. You cannot, however, change the beneficiary by naming someone else in your will or living trust. If this should happen, the beneficiary named in the life insurance policy will inherit its proceeds as previously determined. The named beneficiary on the life insurance policy supersedes anyone named in the will, so changes must be made on the policy itself.

If you live in a community property state and buy a life insurance policy with community property money, one-half of the proceeds are owned by the surviving spouse, regardless of whom the policy names.

If you want minor children to be the beneficiaries of your life insurance policy, you need to arrange some means for the money to be supervised by a competent adult. A good way to do this is to leave the proceeds under your state's Uniform Transfers to Minors Act by naming an adult custodian for the minor child's inheritance. (See chapter 5 for more on the UTMA.)

JOINT OWNERSHIP OF PROPERTY

The purpose of holding property in joint ownership is usually to avoid probate. Not all joint ownerships will avoid probate, but for those that do, setting them up is quite simple. You usually don't even have to prepare any additional documents. All you need do is state how you want to hold title, on the paper that shows your ownership: the real estate deed for the house; the certificate of ownership of the car; the passbook or the registration card on file at the bank; the statement for the brokerage account; and the stock certificates or bonds for individual stocks or bonds. It's easy, it's not expensive, and it's possible to do without a lawyer. If you are unclear as to how you hold title, look at how the names are listed on the title documents.

There are a number of ways to own property with someone else, not all of which will avoid probate. Most, however, will. (For more information on joint ownership, see chapter 2.)

METHODS OF JOINT OWNERSHIP

METHODS OF HOLDING TITLE	AVOIDS PROBATE?
1. Joint tenancy with right of survivorship	Yes
2. Tenancy by the entirety	Yes
3. Community property* (Arizona, California, Idaho, Nevada, New Mexico, Texas, Washington, and Wisconsin)	No, except in California, and in New Mexico under certain circumstances
4. Community property with right of survivorship*	Yes, but only in Arizona, Nevada, Texas, and Wisconsin
5. Tenancy in common	No

Joint Tenancy

The Facts

Joint tenancy is one of the simplest probate avoidance methods, because all property held in joint tenancy carries with it the right of survivorship. Therefore, when one joint tenant dies his ownership share of the joint tenancy property automatically transfers to, and becomes the property of, the surviving joint tenant(s), without the need for any probate proceeding.

*Married couples only.

The automatic transfer to the surviving joint tenant is inherent in this form of ownership. Therefore, you *must* leave your interest in the joint property to your other joint tenant. If you name someone else in your will, the will document will have no effect.

You may terminate a joint tenancy. The property then converts into a tenancy in common, in which each tenant can now transfer or leave their share of the property to anyone they so choose.

Any number of joint tenants can hold ownership to property, but they must all own equal shares. Everyone shares equally in income, profits, and losses from the property. If an ownership document gives a different percentage of shares to different joint tenants, the property is a tenancy in common, and there are no survivorship rights for the co-owner(s). Property held in a tenancy in common does *not* avoid probate on its own. To avoid probate with a tenancy in common, each owner can put his share of the property into a living trust.

Although real estate is commonly held in joint tenancy, it is not the only commodity with ownership in this manner: bank accounts; automobiles, boats, planes; brokerage accounts; and individual stocks and bonds are only some of the property routinely held in joint tenancy for the very purpose of avoiding probate.

How to Take Title in Joint Tenancy

Joint tenancy is available in all states with the exception of the following six states, which have limited or abolished joint tenancy as described:

1. Alaska—No joint tenancy in real estate, except for husband and wife, who may own as tenants by the entirety.
2. North Carolina—No joint tenancy for any property except joint bank accounts.
3. Pennsylvania—No joint tenancy in real estate, but allowed for personal property.
4. South Carolina—Real estate joint tenancy must include the words "with right of survivorship."
5. Tennessee—No joint tenancy for any property except for husband and wife, who may own as tenants by the entirety.
6. Texas—No joint tenancy in any property unless there is an agreement in writing between joint owners.

To create a joint tenancy, pay attention to how you and the other co-owners are listed on the title document. Some salespeople may tell you that by connecting the names of the owners with the word "or," not "and," you have created a joint tenancy. Maybe yes and maybe no. To avoid ambiguity and confusion later, call yourselves "joint tenants with the right of survivorship," or write the abbreviation JTWRS clearly after your names.

Joint Tenancy

PROS	CONS
It's easy to create.	The last surviving joint tenant must use another method to avoid probate at his death.
It's easy for the survivor to transfer title to himself.	
It works for just about everything you own: cars, real estate, bank accounts, and more.	Probate is not avoided if owners die simultaneously.
The survivor doesn't have to worry about creditors' claims. After one owner dies, joint tenancy property is subject only to claims for debts that are the joint responsibility of both joint tenants.	Importance of "JTWRS."
	The shares of each owner must be equal.
	Not available for some kinds of property in some states.
You can have as many joint tenants as you want, as long as each owns an equal share.	If you want to add another tenant to your sole ownership, you must give the cotenant a full one-half ownership interest.

Joint Tenancy Bank Accounts

Most forms of bank accounts can be owned in joint tenancy, including checking, savings, and certificates of deposit. To open such an account, everyone involved signs as joint tenants with right of survivorship. When one joint tenant dies, the survivor(s) gain access to the account, with no need to go through probate.

Some states have laws spelling out the legal consequences of joint accounts. But most states leave it to the persons who create the account to define the rights of the joint holders, in an agreement signed when the account is opened. Joint bank accounts generally fall into one of three basic categories:

1. Joint tenancy with immediate vesting—Each joint owner, on the creation of the account, acquires an interest in one-half of the funds deposited, and neither can withdraw more than one-half without the consent of the other.
2. Revocable account—Each can withdraw the full amount on deposit without the consent of the other. Avoid using this type of account unless you have total faith in the honesty of your cotenant.
3. Convenience account—One person deposits all the funds and has the sole right to the funds while both are alive. The other can make deposits and withdrawals only as "agent" for the other.

All three types provide for survivorship, with the property automatically inherited by the surviving owner. All three types also spare your surviving owner the hassle and inconvenience of probate.

Joint Tenancy Safe-Deposit Boxes

A joint tenancy safe-deposit box can be a sensible place to keep important personal documents. Either joint tenant can obtain access to the documents when needed. In states with inheritance taxes, safe-deposit boxes are usually sealed by the bank as soon as it receives notification of the owner's death. The contents cannot be released until the box is inventoried by a government official or a waiver is obtained—usually a relatively simple procedure.

Tenancy by the Entirety

Tenancy by the entirety is only for married couples. When one spouse dies, his interest in the property automatically transfers to the surviving spouse by the entirety. The transfer avoids probate and the survivor inherits the property quickly and without the irritation of lawyers. The states that allow tenancy by the entirety ownership are:

Alaska	Maryland	Oklahoma
Arkansas	Massachussetts	Oregon*
Delaware	Michigan*	Pennsylvania
District of Columbia	Mississippi	Rhode Island
Florida	Missouri	Tennessee
Hawaii	New Jersey	Vermont
Illinois*	New York*	Virginia
Indiana*	North Carolina*	Wyoming
Kentucky*	Ohio†	

If property is held in tenancy by the entirety, neither spouse can transfer his half of the property while alive or by will or trust. The deceased spouse *must* pass it to the surviving spouse. Tenancy by the entirety property is well protected from creditors, since it is usually subject only to claims for debts that are the joint responsibility of both spouses. One spouse's creditors cannot attach the property owned by both parties. Moreover, if one spouse in a tenancy by the entirety files for bankruptcy, creditors can't reach or sever the property that's held in that manner.

TENANCY BY THE ENTIRETY

PROS	CONS
* It's easy to create.	* Probate is avoided only when the first spouse dies. The survivor must use another method to avoid probate at his death.
* It's easy to transfer title to the surviving spouse.	
* Tenancy by the entirety property is usually subject only to claims for debts that are the joint responsibility of both spouses.	* Probate is not avoided if the spouses die simultaneously.
	* Each spouse owns 50%.
	* It is only available in some states, and in certain of these states it is limited to real estate property.

* Allowed only for real estate.
† Only if created before April 4, 1985.

Tenancy in Common

A tenancy in common is another form of joint tenancy that permits each owner to dispose of his share independently, whenever and to whomever he so chooses. When one owner dies, his share will pass on to his beneficiaries rather than to his joint owner(s). *Tenancy in common property, left on its own, must go through probate.* To get around probate, the property can be transferred to a living trust, which will avoid probate and provide the survivorship feature.

TENANCY IN COMMON

PROS

* A tenant can sell or give away his portion of the property at any time.

* The percentage of ownership can be any amount.

* It is easy to create and easy to transfer.

CONS

* Probate is *not* avoided.

* The tenants and their property are subject to all claims by creditors.

Community Property

If you are married and live in a community property state, most property acquired by you and your spouse during the marriage is automatically community property, unless you signed an agreement to the contrary. Your earnings are community property, and so is everything you buy with your earnings.

Coincidentally, the law doesn't require community property to go to the surviving spouse after the other spouse dies. Each spouse is free to leave *his* half-interest in the community property to someone else. But here is the hitch. If community property isn't left to the remaining spouse, it goes through probate. Keep it in the marital nest, and your property will transfer cost-free and without delay. Leave it to someone outside the marriage duo and it's no longer protected.

Community Property with the Right of Survivorship

You may be able to take advantage of an option that lets you avoid probate completely for community property if you live in Arizona, Nevada, Texas, or Wisconsin. These four states allow couples to add the right of survivorship to their community property—the result being that when one spouse dies, the remaining spouse automatically owns the community property.

Just how you can turn plain community property into right of survivorship community property depends on state law. In Arizona, Nevada, and Wisconsin, one simply needs to put the right words on the title document, just as you would for joint tenancy property. In Texas, you and your spouse need to write up and sign a separate agreement. Spouses are free to change their minds and remove the survivorship provision later, but it must be done in writing.

COMMUNITY PROPERTY WITH RIGHT OF SURVIVORSHIP

PROS	CONS
* It's easy to hold title this way.	* The surviving spouse's estate has to pass through the probate system (except in Wisconsin).
* It's easy to transfer title to the surviving spouse.	
* It works for everything a married couple owns.	* Probate is avoided only in Arizona, Nevada, Texas, and Wisconsin.

Regular Community Property

Of the community property states that don't offer community property with right of survivorship, California is the only one to offer worthwhile probate avoidance directed to community property. Idaho, Washington, and New Mexico have a long way to go.

California does allow community property to pass outside of probate, by two different procedures. For real estate, the spouse simply files a one-page affidavit, or sworn statement, with the county recorder's office. The affidavit supports the spouse's entitlement to full ownership of the house. For property other than real estate, the spouse requests a spousal property offer from the probate court, which then will authorize the transfer into the surviving spouse's name.

Idaho and Washington offer no probate shortcuts for community property. It goes through probate the same as everything else. If you're interested, look for other probate avoidance techniques, such as a living trust, the panacea for all those troubles.

New Mexico allows a surviving spouse to take title to a home held in community property without probate. Unfortunately, there are limitations. It is allowed only after a six-month waiting period, *but only if* (1) all debts and taxes have been paid and (2) probate wasn't necessary for any other assets.

REGULAR COMMUNITY PROPERTY
(NO RIGHT OF SURVIVORSHIP)

PROS	CONS
* It's easy to create.	* No probate avoidance except in California, and in New Mexico under certain circumstances.
* It can apply to anything a couple owns: cars, real estate, bank accounts, stocks, and more.	* Even in California, the surviving spouse must use another method to avoid probate.

Lifetime Gifts

Lifetime gifts don't require you to be selfless. There's a lot in it for you *and* your beneficiaries. Lifetime gifts are a significant way to avoid taxes and probate as well. The tax that people are trying to avoid here is the federal "unified gift and estate tax." This tax, which starts at 37% and rapidly increases to 55%, applies if:

1. you give away more than the amount of estate tax exemption in taxable gifts during your lifetime (tax-free gifts are discussed below); or

2. the value of the taxable property at your death, in addition to the taxable gifts you made during your lifetime, are more than

the estate tax exemption. Remember that property left to your spouse or a tax-exempt charity is not taxable.

The estate tax exemption is laid out by year and amount in the beginning of chapter 13. This is the exemption that is $650,000 for 1999, going up gradually to $1,000,000 in 2006 and beyond. If your estate is large enough to be subjected to estate taxes when you die, giving property away now may bring you under the exempted amount when you die. Therefore, the careful use of annual exclusions can enable you to transfer large assets from your estate, avoiding or reducing taxes, and avoiding probate for these assets as well.

One note of caution: Once you give the property away it is gone for good. Assets you give away must be assets you can live without. If you can manage without them, however, you will have the added pleasure during your lifetime of seeing your gifts help those people and organizations that you love and respect.

Tax-Free Gifts

The following gifts are exempt from a gift tax:

1. the gift tax exclusion of $10,000 per year per person;
2. direct payment for certain educational and medical expenses;
3. gifts of unlimited amount to your spouse; and
4. unlimited donations to tax-exempt charities.

The Gift Tax Exclusion of $10,000
Per Year Per Person

Every taxpayer can give away up to $10,000 in gifts to any one recipient in any calendar year without needing to file a gift tax return. There is *no limit to the number of gifts of $10,000* you can make each year, as long as you don't give more than $10,000 to any one individual. You can also give $10,000 every year *to the same person*.

Here's an example of how this works. Adrienne is in her mid-70s. She is not in good health and is interested in getting money out of her estate for tax purposes and avoiding probate when she dies. She wants to give her single son, David, the down payment for a business he is hoping to buy next year. David excitedly tells his mother the plans over a Thanksgiving turkey. David is Adrienne's only child and she is leaving everything to him.

Adrienne takes advantage of the $10,000 exemption and writes David a check for that amount on December 1, 2000. She writes him an additional check for $10,000 on June 15, 2001. David buys the business and Adrienne begins taking a new prescription drug for her illness. She feels ever so much better with the new medication and lives for another ten years. Doctors credit Adrienne's longevity not only to her new medication, but also to the pleasure she receives from seeing David so happy with his work.

You are also allowed by the IRS to *double* the value of the gift. This means that, *if you are married,* you and your spouse can give up to $20,000 to any individual in any calendar year. Moreover, if you give money to *another couple, that's $40,000* tax free in one calendar year. If you miss a calendar year, you cannot go back and claim the exemption.

Here's an example. Adrienne is also blissfully happy in her new marriage to Bud. David subsequently marries his next-door neighbor, Jewel. They have a beautiful daughter named Jennifer. Adrienne and Bud take advantage of their exemption as a couple and give a total of $20,000 a year to David and $20,000 a year to Jewel. They also give Jennifer a tax-free gift of $10,000 annually. Since Jennifer is a minor and cannot, by law, own more than a few thousand dollars without adult control, the older couple name David as the custodian and transfer the money to him under the Uniform Transfers to Minors Act. Every year until they both die simultaneously in a sailing accident, Adrienne and Bud give a combined tax-free gift of $40,000 to David and Jewel and a $10,000 tax-free gift, via the UTMA, to Jennifer.

Gifts for Tuition and Medical Bills

If you pay someone else's school tuition or medical bills, the IRS will reward your generosity. *However, in both instances, you MUST pay the money directly to the school or to the medical provider in order to make the gift tax free.* The payments *cannot* go through someone else. If it is not a direct payment to the school or medical provider, the gift will be taxed and a gift-tax return, Form 709, must be filed.

Education Expenses

Wiley decides to pay part of his grandson, Ware's, college tuition this year. He writes a check to his son, Bruce, for $5,000, who deposits the check in his own bank account. After he is sure the check has cleared, Bruce writes a check payable to University of Nevada, Las Vegas for $5,000 and sends it along to Ware's college.

This payment is *not* tax free. Wiley didn't give it directly to UNLV. He gave it to Bruce, who deposited the $5,000 in his checking account. Bruce was the one who paid the tuition directly to the school.

Also, federal law limits what educational expenses are covered. *Tuition is the only educational expense that is covered.* Tuition is what a school charges for education training. You can't make tax-free gifts for lodging, or supplies, including books. Tuition, however, is not limited to higher or academic education. Just about every kind of school, with the exception of some correspondence schools and mail-order mills, are included.

Medical Expenses

Mona and Renee have been friends for a long time. Mona becomes ill, but she refuses to see a doctor because she doesn't have medical insurance and won't be able to pay the medical expenses on her own. Renee is very upset about Mona's situation and insists on paying the medical bills, if Mona will only go to the medical center down the road. Mona resists but eventually sets up appointments. Fortunately, the tests show nothing serious. Mona recovers from the unknown ailment and the medical bills start arriving. Renee sends checks worth a total of $7,000 directly to the doctors and the hospital.

The $7,000 to the doctors and hospital is considered a tax-free gift to Mona. Renee paid the bills *directly,* bypassing Mona completely. Had Mona paid for the medical expenses herself and then been reimbursed by Renee, the gift would *not* have passed tax free. Instead, the bills were correctly and directly paid to the providers.

Federal law also limits what medical bills are covered. You can pay tax free for:

1. the diagnosis, treatment, or prevention of disease;
2. transportation that is essential to these services;
3. insurance covering this medical care; and
4. lodging up to $50 a night.

Cosmetic surgery is *not* covered, unless it is necessary because of a disfiguring illness or injury.

Unlimited Gifts to Your Spouse

All gifts you make to your spouse are tax free as long as your spouse is a United States citizen. If he is not a citizen, a tax-free gift is limited to $100,000 per year.

Unlimited Donations to Charities

All gifts you make to a tax-exempt charity are tax free. If you are unsure about whether the organization is tax exempt, ask someone who works there. If you receive literature on the organization, you can read how it is designated. A tax-exempt charity will be designated a 501(c)(3) organization. Gifts to a 501(c)(4) organization are *not* exempt from the gift tax.

Exemptions for Small Estates

There is always the possibility that you can take advantage of special procedures for small estates. This information is covered in chapter 11.

Living Trusts

Living trusts are so important and so popular that I have given them a separate chapter (chapter 13).

Fortunately, the American public now has other ways to pass property than by will alone. The big advantage to avoiding probate is that you avoid lawyers and, as surely as one follows the other, hefty expenses. Generally speaking, when you go to a lawyer and say you want to make out a will, that is what you get—a will. Very rarely will an attorney volunteer ways to dispose of your belongings in a manner more advantageous to *you*. The will, followed by the inevitable probate process, is advantageous to *them*. The public, however, is catching on. The devices you have learned about in this chapter and the living trust, a discussion of which follows, take control from the lawyers and place it where it rightfully belongs: in your hands and in the hands of your beneficiaries.

13

Avoiding Probate
with a Living Trust

*Those who go to an attorney and merely ask for a will may get
less, and pay more, than they bargained for.*

—*A Report on Probate: Consumer Perspectives and Concerns,*
commissioned by the American Association of Retired Persons (1990)

The living trust is probably the most important and flexible estate planning device available today. It holds all of your assets both during
your life and after your death. Here is how it works: *When you set up
your living trust, you transfer the title of all your assets (real estate, stocks,
bonds, etc.) from your name to the name of the trust. You then name
yourself as the trustee as well as the beneficiary.* That gives you, and only
you, total and complete control of all your assets during your lifetime.
Even though you have relinquished *ownership* of your assets, you will
retain *control* of those same assets. You can buy, sell, transfer, borrow—
whatever you want, just as you do now. A sample Declaration and Instrument of a Living Trust for One Person is provided in the appendix.

*Here is the real benefit: A living trust avoids probate. It avoids the ex-
pense of probate and the delay between the date of death and the final
distribution of property. The probate process covers only those assets that
are solely in your name.* Assets held in a living trust at the time of your
death are not subject to probate because they are not legally "owned"
by you. Property left under a will must go through probate, but property in a living trust goes directly to your beneficiaries. They will have
total control, without interference from the courts.

Living Trust Terms

grantor The person who sets up the trust (that's you).

trust document The legal entity that contains all the terms and provision of the trust.

trust property (aka trust principal and trust estate) The property you transfer to the trustee.

trustee The person who has control over the trust property.

successor trustee The person you, the grantor, name to take over as trustee after your death.

beneficiaries You are the beneficiary while you are alive. When you die, these are the people or organizations who will inherit the trust property.

Advantages of the Living Trust

➡ It avoids the expense and delay of probate.

➡ Property can be transferred to beneficiaries without delay.

➡ It enables a going business to continue without the interruption that probate would cause.

➡ A living trust works for most everything you own.

➡ Publicity is avoided and the estate assets remain secret. A living trust, unlike a will, is not a matter of public record.

➡ It allows you to watch the trust in operation and make changes before you die and the trust becomes irrevocable.

➡ It permits you to name alternate beneficiaries, unlike most other probate-avoiding devices. Alternate beneficiaries are the people who will inherit if your first choice dies before you do.

➡ You can amend or revoke the trust at any time.

➡ It can avoid family disputes because relatives do not have to be notified of your death.

➡ It brings together real estate assets in two or more states or countries and avoids additional probate and administration of the estate in places where the property is located.

➡ A living trust is less vulnerable to attack than a will.

➡ It is more difficult for creditors to reach your assets than with a will.

➡ It provides for the management of assets for an incompetent person. Rather than the court appointing a guardian, a trustee or successor trustee can immediately step in for the incompetent person and manage the assets of the trust.

➡ Spouses can make one combined trust.

➡ It is an excellent vehicle for a single person, the elderly, or others who can't rely on family members to handle financial matters in the event of a disability.

Protection Against Incapacity

The living trust is an excellent method of protecting your assets in the event of incapacity. Without a living trust and without a durable power of attorney for finances, if you become mentally incapacitated before you die, the probate court will appoint someone to take control of your trust assets and financial affairs. These court-appointed financial guardians must file strict annual accountings with the court. The entire procedure is expensive, time-consuming, and humiliating. (See chapter 10, Planning for Financial Decision-Making if You Become Incompetent.)

A living trust, however, sets forth your instructions in the event you become legally incompetent. Your successor trustee, whose normal job is to take over as trustee *after your death,* will step in and manage trust property *during your lifetime.* Incapacity is determined on the basis of one of two methods:

1. certification by two doctors (who are not on the team of the grantor's treating physicians) who would attest to the lack of capacity of the grantor; or
2. the existence of a court order certifying the incapacity of the grantor.

It is important to note that you should still sign a durable power of attorney for financial management, since your successor trustee has no authority to manage property outside of your trust. In this document, you can authorize your successor trustee, or anyone else you choose, to make financial decisions for *nontrust property* if you become incompetent. For example, you may opt to not put your checking account in the trust. Or, you may receive a tax refund or win money in litigation. If you become incompetent and have not signed a durable power of attorney, the court will appoint a stranger to pay your bills. The types of property that are commonly put in and kept out of a living trust are discussed below.

More Protection from Court Challenges

There is more protection against attack with a living trust for two reasons:

1. Courts have more consistently protected living trusts from attack than challenges to wills. It is much more difficult for a disgruntled relative to prove incapacity, fraud, or undue influence in the establishment of the trust, due to your continuing involvement with the management of the trust.

2. Living trusts do not require that notice be given to family members of your death. Thus, time can go by before they are aware of your death or the existence of the trust. The fact that probate will not delay the distribution of assets means that your property may already be distributed long before your relatives realize that a challenge could have been made.

Multiple Probate Proceedings

Avoiding probate is particularly important if you own real estate in more than one state. With a will, you must file with the probate court in not only the state in which you live, but *also* in any other state where your real estate is located. This serves to double or even triple the cost, the delay, and the annoyance of the probate process. On the other hand, a living trust will consolidate these state proceedings—and guarantee that your relatives will bless you!

Assuring Privacy of the Estate

The living trust is not registered anywhere. It is a confidential document. The only people with a right to see the trust document are the trustee and, eventually, the successor trustee. Not even the beneficiaries have a right to see the document. A will, by contrast, is a matter of public record.

DISADVANTAGES OF A LIVING TRUST

➡ A living trust is more expensive to create, if you go to a lawyer, than is a will. A living trust can cost upward of $1,000, while a will is around $500. These expenses would involve, primarily, the cost of transferring your property to the trust, but they are well worth it compared to the costs of probating a will. There are no maintenance costs.

➡ If you fail to transfer property to the trust, you leave it vulnerable to probate.

➡ You will prevail, but you may run into resistance if you want to refinance property in a trust.

➡ Some states charge a transfer tax for placing real estate in a trust, but it is minimal in comparison to probate fees.

DOES EVERYONE REALLY NEED A LIVING TRUST?

No. While the living trust is the most important means of avoiding probate and is legal in every state, not everyone really needs one. First, some people don't need a plan, at this time, to avoid probate. Second, even if you do want to avoid probate, there may be other equally efficient and simpler ways, at this particular point, to do so.

You may *not* need a living trust now if you fall within one of the following categories:

1. Your primary goals are to provide for the financial and physical well being of your children. If you are young, healthy, and not particularly affluent, a will may be better for you at this time. You will need a will to appoint a guardian of the person and a guardian of the finances for minor children. Life insurance can insure money for the children. Later on, when you have accumulated more property, you can create a living trust.

2. Your current situation is such that other probate-avoiding devices would be cheaper and easier to use. In addition, the laws of some states allow that certain amounts or types of property can be transferred, especially to a spouse, without probate by use of a will. Assets valued un-

der a certain amount at death can also escape probate. (See chapter 11 on exemptions for small estates.)

3. You or your business have a serious debt problem and a lot of creditors are looking for you. Probate provides that if a notified creditor does not file a claim against you within a few months, he is out of luck and you are home free. A living trust, on the other hand, does not create any such cutoff time, so your assets can be subject to future claims from creditors for a much longer period.

4. You already hold property in joint tenancy, tenancy by the entirety, or, in some states, community property. If you are married, it is likely that you hold property in a manner that already avoids probate.

THE BASICS OF A LIVING TRUST

A trust is a legal entity created to control the distribution of property. A trust that holds assets and distributes them to your beneficiaries, while avoiding probate, is called a revocable living trust or an inter vivos trust, since you create it during your lifetime. You can create one by preparing and signing a document called a declaration (or instrument) of trust. You and your spouse can even create one trust, together.

The trust document, similar to a will, states who you want to inherit your property. Once you sign the document and transfer your property into the trust, your trust becomes the legal "owner" of that property. *Your trust will operate or have effect only as to that property that has been actually transferred to the trust.*

Even though the trust now "owns" the property, for all practical purposes it is as if you still owned it. Creditors can look to the trust for debts and the government can still assess it for income and estate taxes. You are the trustee during your lifetime and you have complete control over the trust property. As the trustee, you can mortgage, give away, or sell the property in the trust, put property in or take property out of the trust, and otherwise control it as you did when you owned the property.

You designate a successor trustee in the trust document to take over upon your incapacity or death, at which time the trust becomes irrevocable. The successor trustee immediately steps in, and has the same power to buy, sell, or transfer the assets, and to use them and distribute them as you would have wanted them to be used or distributed. In most cases, the whole process of distributing the assets can be handled *in a few weeks at little or no cost*—because there is no probate.

If you left real estate in your trust to your Aunt Tillie, the successor trustee can simply sign a deed transferring the property from the trust to your aunt. With property like brokerage accounts or bank accounts, the successor trustee must show the institution that he has the legal right to take possession of the property. On occasion, the institution will demand more proof that the trust was validly created and never revoked. The successor trustee should produce the original, signed, and notarized trust document, along with his own notarized statement that the trust is in working order.

After the successor trustee has transferred all the property to the beneficiaries outright or placed it in another trust—whatever you requested in the trust document—the living trust ceases to exist.

CREATING A LIVING TRUST

There are two crucial steps in creating a valid living trust:

1. preparing the living trust document; and
2. transferring title or property from your name to the name of your trust. This transfer process is also called "funding the trust."

Preparing the Document

There is no such thing as a *standard* living trust document, although sample language is available in the appendix. A lawyer is *not* needed to prepare one and legalese does *not* have to be used. Lawyers usually charge upward of $1,000 to prepare a living trust. You, however, can draft this document yourself with the help of this book. Even if you decide to use a lawyer and pay the fee, your chances of being satisfied are greater if you are an educated consumer.

A simple document, written in plain English, is all you need to:

➡ name the trustee and the successor trustee;
➡ name the beneficiaries and list the trust property on one or more "schedules" attached to the main trust document;

- identify property in such a way that the successor trustee and the beneficiary know without a doubt what property you are referring to;
- sign the document in front of a notary public (no witnesses are required); and
- keep it in a safe, accessible place where your successor trustee has access to it after your death. It does not need to be filed with the court.

Transferring Trust Property into the Trust's Name

It is essential that you legally transfer into the trust all of the property listed in the trust document. The most common estate planning mistake is having a trust and then failing to put the property into it. The trust MUST be funded. A trust is funded when property is transferred to it. Funding is the legal move that actually puts the trust into effect. From this point on, the property will be administered and distributed according to the terms of your trust, because it is now *in* the trust, with you acting as trustee.

If the trust is not funded, the trust document is useless and all the assets go through probate. They will pass under the terms of your will. If you have no will, they will go to your closest relatives under your state's intestate succession law. If you have no close relatives, your assets will go to the government.

Items with Title (Ownership) Documents
You must change the title documents to show that real estate, stocks, mutual funds, bonds (including government securities), money market accounts, bank accounts, corporations, and limited partnerships and partnerships, as well as vehicles, including automobiles, most boats, trucks, motor homes, and airplanes—and any other property with title documents—are now owned by your living trust. For example, if you own a house and you want to put it into your living trust, you must prepare and sign a new deed, transferring ownership from you to your living trust.

Tip:It usually costs nothing or next to nothing to make these transfers. Some places, however, impose heavy transfer and recording taxes. In California, transfers of real estate must be reported on a Preliminary

Change of Ownership form, available at the county recorders' offices, but no fee or tax is required to file the form.

Items Without Title Documents

If an item doesn't have a title document—furniture, appliances, stereo systems, work tools and machinery, electronics, jewelry, silver, books, computers, artwork, cash, collectibles, and many other types of property—listing it in the trust document is enough to transfer it to the trust, with no additional paperwork required. You simply list them on a trust schedule. You can also use a Notice of Assignment form, a document that states that the property listed on it has been transferred to the trust.

PROPERTY THAT BELONGS IN THE LIVING TRUST

Attorney's and appraisal fees generally correspond to the value of the probate items. Since your goal is to avoid probate, special attention should be given to placing high-value items in your living trust, unless they are already covered by another probate-avoiding device.

Real Estate

The most valuable item most people own is their real estate: house, condominium, time-share, or land. You will save your family serious probate costs by transferring all of your real estate into a living trust. Or, you may already co-own real estate in joint tenancy or tenancy by the entirety, in which case there is less incentive to transfer it to a living trust. However, if you own real estate with someone else and there is no right of survivorship, you can transfer just *your interest in the property* to your trust. (See chapter 2 on joint ownership of property.)

TIPS

➥ Co-op apartments—If you own shares in a co-op corporation that owns your apartment, you may run into difficulty with the corporation, who can be reluctant to let a trust own shares. Check the co-op corporation's laws. If necessary, be persuasive. More and more co-ops are becoming familiar, and therefore comfortable, with the concept.

➡ Mobile homes—Laws vary in different states as to when attached mobile homes become real estate. You may need to contact a lawyer.

➡ Leases on real estate—If you own a lease on real estate, that lease is considered an interest in real estate, and can be transferred to the living trust. For example, you may have a ten-year lease on a store and only two years on the lease has run. You can put the remaining eight years in the trust.

➡ Refinancing your mortgage—If the bank resists refinancing a mortgage, show them a copy of your trust document, which gives you, as trustee, the power to borrow against trust property. You can always transfer the property out of the trust and back into your name, and then, after financing, transfer it back into the living trust.

Small Businesses

The death of an owner is a big blow to any business. Probate delays can compound the loss and cause liquidity and management problems for the operation. A living trust is one way to provide for the efficient and effective continuation of the business. It allows the successor trustee to act on your behalf without court approval and to provide for a smooth, solvent transition to the family, the partners, or whoever inherits the business enterprise.

Money Market and Bank Accounts

Money market funds can be easily transferred into your trust. And, since the funds often contain substantial amounts of cash, it is wise to protect them from the claws of probate. It is equally simple to transfer bank accounts into your trust. You simply need to change the paperwork held by the bank, savings and loan, or credit union.

Or, you may decide to use a pay-on-death account, where you can name a beneficiary for the funds in the bank account, while also avoiding probate. The living trust has one advantage over the P.O.D. account, which you might consider: The living trust permits you to choose an alternate beneficiary, whereas the P.O.D. account does not.

Stocks and Securities

You can register stocks and bonds in the name of your living trust, even if you buy and sell them on a fairly consistent basis. All brokers and mutual fund companies can help you consolidate, as they are familiar with the process. All securities in the account are then owned by your living trust. This means you can use your trust to leave the contents of the account to a specific beneficiary. If you want to leave the contents to two or more beneficiaries, you can:

1. create two or more brokerage accounts; or
2. leave the one account to two or more beneficiaries to own together.

As with the bank accounts, you may "wheel and deal" with your stocks without interference. If you become incompetent, your successor trustee may take over, but his wheeling and dealing is subject to more scrutiny by yourself and your beneficiaries.

There is another option. A number of states, thirty-six to be precise, permit ownership of securities to be registered on a transfer-on-death form. In these states, you can name someone to receive the securities, including mutual funds and brokerage accounts, after you die. These accounts also bypass probate. The Uniform Transfers-on-Death Security Registration Act has been adopted in these states:

Alabama	Maryland	Oklahoma
Alaska	Minnesota	Oregon
Arizona	Mississippi	Pennsylvania
Arkansas	Missouri	South Dakota
Colorado	Montana	Tennessee
Connecticut	Nebraska	Texas
Delaware	Nevada	Utah
Florida	New Hampshire	Virginia
Idaho	New Jersey	Washington
Illinois	New Mexico	West Virginia
Iowa	North Dakota	Wisconsin
Kansas	Ohio	Wyoming

Copyrights, Patents, and Royalties

You can transfer your rights to future royalties, copyrights, and patents to your trust by listing them in your trust property schedule. Then transfer your interest in a copyright, patent, or royalty to the trust, using the proper legal forms.

Other Items with Title Property

A living trust is allowed to "own" almost all types of property. If you have a question or are uncertain about how to do it, just ask yourself, "How was the item transferred to me in the first place?" In most cases, you can use the same approach.

Items Without Title Property

If you wish to hold property in your living trust that has no formal title documentation (antiques, furniture, jewelry, silver), it can be done through a simple, written statement by you, describing the property in detail and stating that you are holding them in your trust. In this statement, you may also declare who is to receive the property upon your death. Such a letter might say:

> I hereby declare that I have transferred the following items of property to the Clement Family Trust, dated January 20, 2000, and that I am holding the same, as Trustee, under the terms and conditions of that trust:
> [list and description of property]
> Upon my death, such items shall be divided equally between my two sons. If either predeceases me, all the property shall go to the survivor. If they both survive me and cannot agree upon a division within two months after my death, I direct my successor trustee to sell the remaining items and divide the proceeds equally between my two sons.
>
> Mary D. Clement

PROPERTY THAT DOES NOT BELONG IN A LIVING TRUST

Cash

You *cannot* transfer cash to a living trust no matter how much you want to leave your favorite nephew, Christopher, $5,000. *But* there is more than one way to achieve your goal. In this instance, you can transfer ownership of a cash account—a savings account, money market account, or certificate of deposit—to your living trust, and name Christopher, in the trust document, as the beneficiary.

IRAs, Profit-Sharing Plans, Pensions, and Other Retirement Plans

Assets that have their own beneficiary designations, such as employee benefits, IRAs, Roth IRAs, 401(k) plans, profit-sharing plans, life insurance, pensions, and the like, cannot legally be owned by the trust. Yet they can all avoid probate. You can name a beneficiary to receive the funds in each account when you die. The funds will go directly to the beneficiaries without going through probate. (See chapter 12, Ways to Avoid Probate.)

Your Personal Checking Account

Trying to write a check on a personal checking account that is owned by a revocable living trust can prove difficult at best—especially in rural areas where the benefits of a living trust have not yet become common knowledge. Some people or institutions may refuse to cash the check. Keep your checking account in your own name, and sign a durable power of attorney for finances so your successor trustee can pay bills and make gifts from your account.

Tip: If your account has the money to justify it, consider adding a P.O.D. beneficiary to your account. Whatever is left in the account goes directly to the beneficiary, bypassing probate.

Vehicles

Vehicles can legally be placed in a living trust, but it is not always practical to do so. Having registration and insurance in the trust's name can be confusing to lenders and insurance companies, although as more people become familiar with living trusts it will become easier. Also, the value of most people's car isn't high enough to worry about transferring it to a living trust. However, if you own valuable or antique vehicles, it may be worth your while to ferret out an insurance company that will allow you to transfer them into a living trust. In addition, chapter 12 discusses ways simpler than a living trust to avoid probate for vehicles in California and Missouri.

Naming a Successor Trustee

You *must* name someone in the trust document to manage your trust property if you are alive but mentally incapacitated, and to distribute your assets after you die. You are the trustee now. The person you choose to follow you is the successor trustee. It is a good idea to choose the same person to be the executor of your will and the successor trustee of your trust.

The person you appoint should be reliable, honest, and trustworthy. Great financial expertise is not a requirement for the job. The successor trustee only *distributes the assets*. The only time he would *manage* them is if you became incompetent. Should that situation occur, the successor trustee can get the help he needs from lawyers and accountants, paid for by the trust.

Legally speaking, you may appoint more than one successor trustee to serve at the same time. Practically speaking, this may lead to disagreements and conflicts. You may also name an alternate successor trustee, if the initial one becomes unable, unwilling, or unavailable to continue.

Leaving Trust Property to Minors or Young Adults

Minors are allowed to control only small amounts of property. Therefore, if any beneficiaries of your estate are minors (under 18 in most states), you will need to name someone to manage the property on their behalf. If you fail to do so, the court will appoint a property guardian for you, with all of the time, money, restrictions, and impersonal entanglements that go with legal proceedings. It is far better for you to choose someone you trust and respect, rather than allowing a total unknown, to manage your children's inheritance. (See chapter 5 on leaving assets to minors.)

Furthermore, although you are not required to do so, you may feel that your young adult children need mature supervision of their inheritance past the age of 18. This can be especially true if the amount of money involved is substantial or if the young adult in question is not as mature as you might like. It is a rare 18-year-old who would opt to save for a rainy day when a bright and shiny red convertible down the street is for sale!

There are two main ways to arrange for property management of a living trust for minors and young adults:

1. create child's subtrusts; or
2. name a custodian under the Uniform Transfers to Minors Act.

Create Child's Subtrusts

You can create child's subtrusts in your living trust. The successor trustee (or the surviving spouse, if you created a shared trust) will manage the money, spending it on education, health, and other needs, until the minor reaches whatever age you have designated (18 or older), when the remaining property is turned over to the beneficiary outright.

Name a Custodian Under the Uniform Transfers to Minors Act (UTMA)

If you live in a state that has adopted the UTMA (all states except for Michigan, South Carolina, and Vermont), you can name a custodian to manage the property you leave a minor child, until the child reaches 18 or 21, depending on state law, or up to 25 in Alaska, California, and Nevada. If you don't feel your minor child needs adult supervision beyond what your state law allows, a custodianship is preferable to a child's subtrust because:

➡ banks and other institutions are more familiar with custodianships;

➡ you have more flexibility in naming a different custodian for each child or even grandchild, rather than only being permitted to name the successor trustee of the trust as *trustee for all the children's and grandchildren's subtrusts*. (See chapter 5 for a complete description of the UTMA.)

Tip: Neither the trustee nor the custodian must be supervised by the court. However, if you fail to name one of them for minor children, the court-appointed guardian of the property is subject to the numerous rules and regulations of court supervision.

TAXES AND TRUSTS

Living Trusts and Income Taxes

An individual's living trust will not save you money on income taxes. The IRS will treat your trust property in the same fashion that it treats any other property you own. No separate income tax records or returns are necessary *as long as you are both the grantor and the trustee.* Income from property in the living trust must be reported on your personal income tax return. You don't have to file a separate tax return for the trust.

Living Trusts and Death Taxes

A living trust does not, by itself, reduce federal or state estate taxes. Property you leave in your living trust is considered to be part of your estate. There are two types of death taxes: the federal estate tax and the state inheritance tax. Many states have abolished the state inheritance tax, but the federal estate tax is still with us.

STATES THAT HAVE ABOLISHED THE INHERITANCE TAX

Alabama	Arkansas	District of Columbia
Alaska	California	Florida
Arizona	Colorado	Georgia

Hawaii	Nevada	Vermont
Idaho	New Mexico	Virginia
Illinois	North Dakota	Washington
Maine	Oregon	West Virginia
Massachusetts	Rhode Island	Wisconsin
Michigan	South Carolina	Wyoming
Minnesota	Texas	
Missouri	Utah	

The federal estate tax serves as a tax on your right to transfer property to others at your death. Currently, the federal estate tax rates start at 37% and quickly rise to 55% of every dollar in your estate over the amount of the exemption. The federal government has given every person in the United States an exemption for estate tax purposes. This means that if your estate, at the time of your death, is less than the exemption, there will be no federal estate taxes due. In deciding whether your estate is greater than or less than the exemption, the government includes everything you own—even the face value of your life insurance policy. The amount varies, depending on the year of death, as shown below. In addition to the personal exemption, all property left to a spouse who is a U.S. citizen, or to a tax-exempt charity, is exempt from estate taxes.

THE PERSONAL ESTATE TAX EXEMPTION

Year of Death	Exempt Amount (individual)	Exempt Amount (couples)
1998	$625,000	$1,250,000
1999	$650,000	$1,300,000
2000–2001	$675,000	$1,350,000
2002–2003	$700,000	$1,400,000
2004	$850,000	$1,700,000
2005	$950,000	$1,900,000
2006 and after	$1,000,000	$2,000,000

An individual's living trust designed to avoid probate can, however, be combined with a second trust designed to save on taxes. This popular tax-saving trust for couples is called the "marital life estate trust" or AB trust. *Couples can use this trust to shield a combined estate worth be-*

tween $1,250,000 and $2,000,000 from estate taxes, depending on the years of death. The AB trust works like this: A couple creates a trust together and transfers property into it. When the first spouse dies, the trust property goes to the children, avoiding probate—with the restriction that the surviving spouse can use the income of the property during his lifetime. When he subsequently dies, the property in the trust goes to the children outright.

The tax-saving value of AB trusts occurs at the death of the surviving spouse. The first spouse's Trust A and that spouse's own property are subject to the estate tax. The surviving spouse's Trust B assets pass to the remaining beneficiaries of the Trust B without any federal estate tax. If done correctly, the AB trusts will reduce the size of the surviving spouse's estate and thereby limit the future tax liability.

If the value of your estate, or the combined value of your and your spouse's estate, exceeds the estate tax exemption, you will need estate tax planning that this book does not provide. The AB trust is a technical document and also beyond the scope of the book. I include it here to introduce you to the concept and alert you to the possibility that you may want to create one with the help of a lawyer.

Tax ID Numbers

When you are opening accounts or transferring property to your trust and you are asked for a tax identification number, *you may use your own Social Security number.* This is because the trust is considered a "grantor" trust under the tax laws, meaning that all of the trust income and losses are reported on your individual tax return. You will use your Social Security number on all trust accounts and report all dividends, interest, capital gains, or any other trust income (or losses) on your regular 1040 return as you normally would without the trust. The only time you need apply to the IRS for a separate trust ID number (and this is not difficult) is if neither you nor your spouse is a trustee of the trust.

AMENDING OR REVOKING A LIVING TRUST DOCUMENT

I said in the beginning of this chapter that one of the most attractive features of a revocable living trust is its flexibility.

If you have an individual living trust, you may change the terms or end the whole trust, at any time.

If you have a shared living trust with your spouse:

1. either spouse can revoke the living trust;
2. both spouses must consent in writing to change a trust provision—to change, for example, a successor trustee or beneficiary;
3. both spouses must consent in writing to transfer real estate out of the trust; and
4. buyers and title insurance companies require both spouses' signatures on transfer documents.

After one spouse dies, the surviving spouse:

1. can amend the terms of the trust document that deal with his property; and
2. cannot change the terms of the document that determine what happens to the *deceased spouse's* trust property.

Times When You May Want to Amend a Living Trust

➡ You get married.
➡ You give birth to each new child.
➡ A child dies.
➡ A child becomes disabled and needs long-term care.
➡ You add valuable property.
➡ You get rid of valuable property.
➡ You change your mind about beneficiaries and alternate beneficiaries.
➡ You change your mind about who will serve as the successor trustee.
➡ You move from a common law state to a community property state and vice versa.
➡ Your spouse dies.
➡ A major beneficiary or a major alternate beneficiary dies.

Times When You May Want to Revoke a Living Trust

➡ Such massive revisions are needed to the terms of the trust that to only amend the document would risk inconsistencies, ambiguities, and confusion.

➡ You and your spouse get divorced.

WHY YOU STILL NEED A WILL

A living trust does *not* eliminate the need for a will. You will need a backup will to do the following:

1. Transfer property to your living trust that was not transferred before your death. This is usually accomplished by a simple pour-over will, which provides that any remaining property be poured over into your living trust. Unfortunately, this property must still go through probate on its way to your trust.
2. Designate beneficiaries for any property you haven't already transferred to your living trust or other probate-avoiding device.
3. Designate guardians of the person and of the property for minor children, which can only be designated in a will.
4. If you are involved in litigation in any way and may be awarded monetary damages.
5. Disinherit someone.
6. Forgive debts owed to you by others.

It is impossible to overestimate the importance of estate planning. You've worked hard to build up an estate of which you and your family can be proud. Now you can make sure that your assets will be used to best provide for *you,* during your lifetime, and subsequently for your beneficiaries. The main method of safeguarding your assets is to keep them, and all documents relating to them, away from lawyers. You can successfully accomplish this now. You know all you really need to know about wills to make one on your own, you are aware of the various legal devices in place to avoid a time-consuming and costly probate process, and you have learned how to avoid court-appointed guardians if you become mentally incapacitated. You now know how to successfully die without a lawyer!

PART V

Appendix
Estate Planning
Documents

1. Sample Wills

   a. Standard Sample Last Will and Testament
   b. Sample Will for a Married Person with No Minor Children
   c. Will in Which You Include Your Own Personal Will Clauses
   d. Personal Will Clauses

2. Self-Proving Affidavit

3. Codicil

4. Durable Power of Attorney for Finances

5. New York Living Will

6. New York Health Care Proxy

7. New York Nonhospital Do-Not-Resuscitate Order

8. Declaration and Instrument of a Living Trust for One Person

STANDARD SAMPLE LAST WILL AND TESTAMENT

of

_____

I, _____,

also known as _____,

a resident of the _____ of _____,

which I do declare to be my place of domicile, being of sound and disposing mind and memory, do hereby make, publish, and declare this to be my Last Will and Testament, thus revoking all Wills and Codicils to Wills previously made by me.

FIRST (Debt Clause): I direct that the Executor (Executrix) hereinafter named pursuant to this Last Will and Testament, pay (as soon after my death as practical) all of my just debts and obligations, including funeral expenses and the expenses incident to my last illness, but excepting those long-term debts secured by real or personal property that may be assumed by the person designed to receive such property.

SECOND (Distribution Clause): I give, devise, and bequeath unto the herein named persons, that portion or that particular property of my estate, whether real property or personal property, of whatsoever kind of character, and wherever situation, as follows:

_____

_____

_____

_____

THIRD (Common Disaster Clause): If my spouse, if any, shall die as a result of a common disaster with me, then my spouse shall be deemed to have (*check one*): ❒ survived me (❒ predeceased me).

FOURTH (Executor [Executrix] Appointment Clause): I hereby nominate, constitute, and appoint as the Executor (Executrix) of my Estate: _____,

provided, however, that in the event he (she) is unable or unwilling to so serve in such capacity, then I nominate, constitute, and appoint _____.

FIFTH (Guardian Appointment Clause): I hereby nominate, constitute, and appoint as the Guardian of any minor child(ren) of mine: _____,

provided, however, that in the event he(she) is unable or unwilling to serve in that capacity, then I nominate, constitute, and appoint _____.

SIXTH (Saving Clause): In the event any separate provision of this Last Will and Testament is held to be invalid by a Court of competent jurisdiction, then such finding shall not invalidate this entire Last Will and Testament, but only the subject provision.

IN WITNESS WHEREOF, I have hereunto signed this, my Last Will and Testament, this _____

day of _____, 20 _____, in the _____ of _____,

State of _____.

_____

Testator (Testatrix)

(continued on next page)

(STANDARD SAMPLE LAST WILL AND TESTAMENT continued from previous page)

The foregoing Last Will and Testament was on the above date, subscribed, sealed, published, and declared by the Testator (Testatrix), above named, as his(her) Last Will and Testament in the presence of each of us below named Witnesses, and at the same time, we at his(her) request in his(her) presence and in the presence of each other who hereunto subscribed our names as witnesses hereto; this Attestation Clause having been first read aloud and we hereby certify that at the time of the execution hereof, we believe the Testator(Testatrix) to be of sound and disposing mind and memory.

_____ of _____
address

_____
city   state

_____ of _____
address

_____
city   state

_____ of _____
address

_____
city   state

SELF-PROVING AFFIDAVIT

State of _____)

County of _____)ss.

WE, _____ , _____ ,

and _____ , the witnesses whose names are signed to the attached or foregoing instrument, being first duly sworn, do hereby declare to the undersigned authority that the testator(testatrix) signed and executed the foregoing instrument as his(her) Last Will and Testament, that he(she) had signed willingly (or willingly directed another to sign for him(her), that he(she) executed it as his(her) free and voluntary act for the purposes therein expressed; that each of the witnesses, in the presence of each other and hearing of the testator(testatrix), signed the Last Will and Testament as witnesses; and that to the best of their knowledge, the testator(testatrix) was at the time eighteen years of age or older, of sound mind, and under no constraint or undue influence.

_____   _____
Witness Signature   Witness Signature

_____
Witness Signature

SUBSCRIBED AND SWORN to before me this _____ day of _____ , 20 ___.

My Commission expires: _____   _____
Notary Public

Note 1. This Affidavit merely self-proves the Last Will and Testament in the event all of the Witnesses are unavailable when the Will is probated. It is not, therefore, required to validate this Will, but only an option (see Note 2).

Note 2. This Last Will and Testament is a witnessed Will which means it will not be valid unless it is witnessed (signed) by the number of witnesses required under State Laws who do not have an interest in the estate of the person making this Last Will and Testament.

SAMPLE WILL FOR A MARRIED PERSON WITH NO MINOR CHILDREN

Will of _____ [your name]

I, _____ [your name], a resident of _____ [city], _____ [county], _____ [state], declare that this is my will.

1. **Revocation of Prior Wills.** I revoke all wills and codicils that I have previously made.

2. **Personal Information.** I am a single adult.

3. **Children,** I have _____ [number] _____ [child/children] whose name(s) and date(s) of birth _____ [is/are]:
   _____ [name]   _____ [date of birth]
(repeat as needed)

There _____ [is/are] _____ [number] living child-children of my deceased child_____ [name]:
   _____ [name of grandchild] _____ [date of birth]
(repeat as needed)

If I do not leave property in this will to a child or grandchild listed above, my failure to do so is intentional.

4. **Specific Gifts.** I leave the following specific gifts:
   I leave _____ [description of gift(s)] to _____ [beneficiary/beneficiaries] or, if _____ [she/he/they] _____ [does/do] not survive me, to _____ [alternate beneficiary/beneficiaries].
   I leave _____ [description of gift(s)] to _____ [beneficiary/beneficiaries] or, if _____ [she/he/they] _____ [does/do] not survive me, to _____ [alternate beneficiary/beneficiaries].
(repeat as needed)

5. **Residuary Estate.** I leave my residuary estate, that is, the rest of my property not otherwise specifically and validly disposed of by this will or in any other manner, to _____ [residuary beneficiary/beneficiaries] or, if _____ [she/he/they] _____ [does/do] not survive me, to _____ [alternate residuary beneficiary/beneficiaries].

6. **Beneficiary Provisions.** The following terms and conditions shall apply to the beneficiary clauses of this will.

   A. **45-Day Survivorship Period.** As used in this will, the phrase "survive me" means to be alive or in existence as an organization on the 45th day after my death. Any beneficiary, except any alternate residuary beneficiary, must survive me to inherit under this will.

   B. **Shared Gifts.** If I leave property to be shared by two or more beneficiaries, it shall be shared equally between them unless this will provides otherwise.

   If any beneficiary of a shared specific gift left in a single paragraph of the Specific Gifts clause, above, does not survive me, that deceased beneficiary's portion of the gift shall be given to the surviving beneficiaries in equal shares.

   If any residuary beneficiary of a shared residuary gift does not survive me, that deceased beneficiary's portion of the residue shall be given to the surviving residuary beneficiaries in equal shares.

(continued on next page)

C. **Encumbrances**. All property that I leave by this will shall pass subject to any encumbrances or liens on the property.

7. *Executor.*

A. Nomination of Executor. I nominate _____ [executor's name] as executor, to serve without bond. If _____ [she/he] shall for any reason fail to qualify or cease to act as executor, I nominate _____ [successor executor's name] as executor, also to serve without bond.

B. Executor's Powers. I direct that my executor take all actions legally permissible to have the probate of my will conducted as simply and as free of court supervision as possible, including filing a petition in the appropriate court for the independent administration of my estate.

I grant to my personal representative the following powers, to be exercised as he or she deems to be in the best interests of my estate:

1. To pay, as my executor decides is best (unless state law mandates a specific method for payment), all my debts and taxes, that may, by reason of my death, be assessed against my estate or any portions of it.
2. To retain property without liability for loss or depreciation resulting from such retention.
3. To dispose of property by public or private sale, or exchange, or otherwise, and receive or administer the proceeds as part of my estate.
4. To vote stock, to exercise any option or privilege to convert bonds, notes, stocks, or other securities belonging to my estate into other bonds, notes, stocks, or other securities and to exercise all other rights and privileges of a person owning similar property in his own right.
5. To lease any real property that may at any time form part of my estate.
6. To abandon, adjust, arbitrate, compromise, sue on or defend, and otherwise deal with and settle claims in favor of or against my estate.
7. To continue, maintain, operate, or participate in any business that is a part of my estate, and to effect incorporation, dissolution, or other change in the form of organization of the business.
8. To do all other acts, which in his or her judgment may be necessary or appropriate for the proper and advantageous management, investment, and distribution of my estate.

The foregoing powers, authority, and discretion are in addition to the powers, authority, and discretion vested in him or her by operation of law and may be exercised as often as is deemed necessary or advisable without application to or approval by any court in any jurisdiction.

Signature

I subscribe my name to this will the _____ [day] day of _____ [month], _____ [year], at _____ [city], _____ [county], _____ [state], and do hereby declare that I sign and execute this instrument as my last will and that I sign it willingly, that I execute it as my free and voluntary act for the purposes therein expressed, and that I am of the age of majority or otherwise legally empowered to make a will, and under no constraint or undue influence.

_____ [your signature]

(SAMPLE WILL FOR A MARRIED PERSON WITH NO MINOR CHILDREN continued from previous page)

Witnesses

On this _____ [day] day of _____ [month], _____ [year], _____ [your name] declared to us, the undersigned, that this instrument was _____ [his/her] will and requested us to act as witnesses to it. _____ [He/She] thereupon signed this will in our presence, all of us being present at the same time. We now, at _____ [his/her] request, in _____ [his/her] presence and in the presence of each other, subscribe our names as witnesses and declare we understand this to be _____ [his/her] will, and that to the best of our knowledge the testator is of the age of majority, or is otherwise legally empowered to make a will, and under no constraint or undue influence.

We declare under penalty or perjury that the foregoing is true and correct, this _____ [day] day of _____ [month], _____ [year], at _____ [city and state].

_____ [witness's signature]

_____ [witness's typed name] residing at _____ [address], _____ [city], _____ [county], _____ [state].

_____ [witness's signature]

_____ [witness's typed name] residing at _____ [address], _____ [city], _____ [county], _____ [state].

_____ [witness's signature]

_____ [witness's typed name] residing at _____ [address], _____ [city], _____ [county], _____ [state].

WILL IN WHICH YOU INCLUDE YOUR OWN
PERSONAL WILL CLAUSES

Will of _____ [your name]

I, _____ [your name], a resident of _____ [city], _____ [county], _____ [state], declare that this is my will.

1. *Revocation of Prior Wills.* I revoke all wills and codicils that I have previously made (including the will dated _____ , 20____).

Signature

I subscribe my name to this will the _____ [day] day of _____ [month], _____ [year], at _____ [city], _____ [county], _____ [state], and do hereby declare that I sign and execute this instrument as my last will and that I sign it willingly, that I execute it as my free and voluntary act for the purposes therein expressed, and that I am of the age of majority or otherwise legally empowered to make a will, and under no constraint or undue influence.

_____ [your signature]

Witnesses

On this _____ [day] day of _____ [month], _____ [year], _____ [your name] declared to us, the undersigned, that this instrument was _____ [his/her] will and requested us to act as witnesses to it. _____ [He/She] thereupon signed this will in our presence, all of us being present at the same time. We now, at _____ [his/her] request, in _____ [his/her] presence and in the presence of each other, subscribe our names as witnesses and declare we understand this to be _____ [his/her] will, and that to the best of our knowledge the testator is of the age of majority, or is otherwise legally empowered to make a will, and under no constraint or undue influence.

We declare under penalty of perjury that the foregoing is true and correct, this _____ [day] day of _____ [month], _____ [year], at _____ [city], _____ [county], _____ [state].

_____ [witness's signature]

_____ [witness's typed name] residing at _____ [street address], _____ [city], _____ [county], _____ [state].

_____ [witness's signature]

_____ [witness's typed name] residing at _____ [street address], _____ [city], _____ [county], _____ [state].

_____ [witness's signature]

_____ [witness's typed name] residing at _____ [street address], _____ [city], _____ [county], _____ [state].

PERSONAL WILL CLAUSES

INSTRUCTIONS:

1. Choose any of the following clauses that you wish to include in your will.
2. Number each clause and insert it under "1. Revocation of Prior Wills" as shown in the Sample Will for a Married Person with No Minor Children. For example, "2. Personal Information" and so on.
3. "Signature" and "Witnesses" come after the inserted clauses at the end of the will, as shown in the Sample Wills.

_____ . *Personal Information.* I am married to _____ [spouse's name] and all references in this will to my _____ [husband/wife] are to _____ [him/her]. I have _____ [number] _____ [child/children] now living, whose name(s) and date(s) of birth _____ [is/are]:

_____ [name] _____ [date of birth]
_____ [name] _____ [date of birth]
(repeat as needed)

There _____ [is/are] _____ [number] living _____ [child/children] of my deceased child _____ [name], whose name(s) and date(s) of birth _____ [is/are]:

_____ [name of grandchild] _____ [date of birth]
(repeat as needed)

If I do not leave property to a child or grandchild listed above, my failure to do so is intentional.

_____ . *Disinheritance.* I direct that _____ [name] be disinherited and receive nothing from my estate.
(repeat as needed)

_____ . *Specific Gifts. I leave the following specific gifts:*
I leave _____ [description of gift] to _____ [names(s) of beneficiary or beneficiaries] or, if _____ [she/he/they] _____ [does/do] not survive me, to _____ [name(s) of alternate beneficiary or beneficiaries].
(repeat as necessary)

* Addition 1. Joint Tenancy Property

I leave any interest in joint tenancy property subject to this will to _____ [beneficiary/beneficiaries] or, if _____ [she/he/they] do not survive me, to _____ [alternate beneficiary/beneficiaries].

* Addition 2. Comments About Your Gifts

_____ . *Debts Forgiven.* I forgive my interest in the following _____ [debt/debts], including all interest accrued as of the date of my death:

Person or Organization Owing Debt   Date of Loan

_____   _____
_____   _____

(repeat as needed)

* Addition 1: Explaining Why You Forgave Debts

I forgive the debts owed me by _____ [person or organization owing debt] because _____ [reason].
(repeat as needed)

(continued on next page)

(PERSONAL WILL CLAUSES continued from previous page)

—————— . **Real Estate Encumbrances.** I direct that the gift of real estate, —————— [address or description of property] left to —————— [name(s) of beneficiary/beneficiaries], be made free of all encumbrances on that property at my death, including, but not limited to, any mortgages, deeds of trust, real property taxes and assessments, and estate and inheritance taxes, and that such encumbrances shall be paid by my executor from the assets below, in the order listed:

—————— [description of assets]

(repeat as needed)

—————— . **Personal Property Encumbrances.** I direct that the following gift, —————— [description of gift], left to —————— [beneficiary/beneficiaries], be made free of all loans, liens, debts, or other obligations on that property, and that all such obligations shall be paid by my executor from the assets below, in the order listed:

—————— [assets]

—————— [assets]

(repeat as necessary)

—————— . **Shared Gifts**

A. If I leave property to be shared by two or more beneficiaries, it shall be shared equally between them unless this will provides otherwise.

B. If any beneficiary of a shared specific gift left in a single paragraph of Clause ——————, [number you've assigned to specific gifts clause], Specific Gifts, does not survive me, that deceased beneficiary's portion of the gift shall be given to the surviving beneficiaries in equal shares.

C. If any residuary beneficiary of a shared residuary gift does not survive me, that deceased beneficiary's portion of the residue shall be given to the surviving residuary beneficiaries in equal shares, unless this will provides otherwise.

Standard Residuary Estate Clause

—————— . **Residuary Estate.** I leave my residuary estate, that is, the rest of my property not otherwise specifically and validly disposed of by this will or in any other manner, to —————— [residuary beneficiary/beneficiaries (specify percentages, if desired)] or, if —————— [she/he/they] —————— [does/do] not survive me, to —————— [alternate residuary beneficiary/beneficiaries].

(This clause may be written for more than one residuary beneficiary and/or with two levels of alternate residuary beneficiaries.)

Survivorship Period

* Alternative 1. 45-Day Survivorship Period

—————— . **Survivorship Period.** As used in this will, the phrase "survive me" means to be alive or in existence as an organization on the 45th day after my death. Any beneficiary, except any alternate residuary beneficiary, must survive me to inherit under this will.

* Alternative 2. Other Survivorship Period

—————— . **Survivorship Period.** As used in this will, the phrase "survive me" means to be alive or in existence as an organization on the —————— th day after my death. Any beneficiary, except any alternate residuary beneficiary, must survive me to inherit under this will.

(PERSONAL WILL CLAUSES continued from previous page)

Abatement

* Alternative 1. Abatement First from Residue

_____ . *Abatement.* If my estate is not sufficient to pay in full all gifts of set dollar amounts made in this will, my executor shall first sell personal property, and then real property, in my residuary estate, in the amount necessary to pay these gifts.

* Alternative 2. Abatement Pro Rata from Cash Gifts

_____ . *Abatement.* If my estate is not sufficient to pay in full all gifts of set dollar amounts made in this will, my executor shall make an appropriate pro rata reduction of each cash gift.

Payment of Death Taxes

* Alternative 1. From Specific Assets

_____ . *Payment of Death Taxes.* I direct my executor to pay all estate, inheritance, or other death taxes assessed against my estate, or taxes payable by beneficiaries for property received from my estate, from the following assets, in the order listed: _____ [description of assets].

* Alternative 2. From All Property in Estate

_____ . *Payment of Death Taxes.* I direct that all estate, inheritance, or other death taxes assessed against my estate, or payable by beneficiaries for property received from my estate, be paid out of all the property in my taxable estate, no matter how transferred, on a pro rata basis by or on behalf of the recipients of the property.

_____ . *Payment of Debts.* I direct my executor to pay all debts and expenses of my estate from the assets listed below, in the order listed, except that liens and encumbrances placed on property as security for repayment of a debt or lien pass with that property, unless I specifically provide otherwise in this will: _____ [description of assets].

Executor

* Alternative 1. Sole Executor

_____ . *Executor.* I appoint _____ [executor] as executor. If _____ [executor] shall for any reason fail to qualify or cease to act as executor, I appoint _____ [successor executor], as executor.
No bond shall be required of any executor.

* Alternative 2. More Than One Executor

_____ . *Executors.* I appoint _____ [executors' names] to serve as executors without bond. Each executor may act for my estate. If any of them fail to qualify or cease to serve as executor, the surviving executor(s) shall serve as executor(s), also without bond. If none of them is available to serve, I appoint _____ [successor executor] as executor, to serve without bond.

* Addition 1: Appointing an Ancillary Executor

If an executor is needed in _____ [state where real estate is located], I appoint _____ [ancillary executor's name] to serve as executor there, without bond.

(continued on next page)

(PERSONAL WILL CLAUSES continued from previous page)

Executor's Powers Clause

* Alternative 1. Standard Executor's Powers Clause

_____ . *Executor's Powers.* I direct that my executor take all actions legally permissible to have the probate of my estate done as simply as possible, including filing a petition in the appropriate court for the independent administration of my estate.

I grant to my executor the following powers, to be exercised as my executor deems to be in the best interests of my estate:

a. Except as otherwise provided in this will, my executor shall pay, as my executor decides is best (unless state law requires a specific method for payment), all my debts, and all taxes that may, by reason of my death, be assessed against my estate or any portion of it.

b. To retain property without liability for loss or depreciation resulting from such retention.

c. To dispose of property by public or private sale, or exchange, or otherwise, and receive or administer the proceeds as a part of my estate.

d. To vote stock, to exercise any option or privilege to convert bonds, notes, stocks, or other securities belonging to my estate into other bonds, notes, stocks, or other securities, and to exercise all other rights and privileges of a person owning similar property in his own right.

e. To lease any real property that may at any time form part of my estate.

f. To abandon, adjust, arbitrate, compromise, sue on or defend, and otherwise deal with and settle claims in favor of or against my estate.

g. To continue, maintain, operate, or participate in any business that is a part of my estate, and to effect incorporation, dissolution, or other change in the form or organization of the business.

h. To do all other acts, which in his or her judgment may be necessary or appropriate for the proper and advantageous management, investment, and distribution of my estate.

The foregoing powers, authority, and discretion are in addition to the powers, authority, and discretion vested in him or her by operation of law and may be exercised as often as is deemed necessary or advisable without application to or approval by any court in any jurisdiction.

Alternative 2. Special Executor's Clause for Texas

_____ . *Personal Representative's Powers.* Except as otherwise required by Texas law, I direct that my personal representative shall take no other action in the county court in relation to the settlement of my estate than the probating and recording of this will, and the return of an inventory, appraisement, and list of claims of my estate.

*Personal Guardian

* Alternative 1. Other Parent As First Guardian

_____ . *Personal Guardian.* If at my death any of my children are minors, and a personal guardian is needed, I nominate _____ [personal guardian's name] to be appointed as personal guardian of my minor children. If _____ [she/he] cannot serve as guardian, I nominate _____ [successor personal guardian] to be appointed as personal guardian.
I direct that no bond be required of any personal guardian.

(PERSONAL WILL CLAUSES continued from previous page)

* Addition: Statement of Reasons for Your Choice

I believe it is in the best interest of my _____ [child/children] for _____ [personal guardian's name] to be _____ [his/her/their] personal guardian because _____ [reasons].

* Alternative 2. Guardian in Place of Other Parent

_____ . *Personal Guardian.* If at my death any of my children are minors, I nominate _____ [personal guardian's name] to be appointed as personal guardian of my minor children. If _____ [she/he] cannot serve as guardian, I nominate _____ [successor personal guardian's name] to be appointed as personal guardian.

I direct that no bond be required of any personal guardian.
I believe it is in the best interests of my children for _____ [personal guardian's name] to be their personal guardian, rather than _____ [natural parent's name] because _____ [reasons].

* Alternative 3. Different Personal Guardians for Different Children

_____ . *Personal Guardian.* If at my death any of my children are minors, and a personal guardian is needed:

I nominate _____ [personal guardian's name] to be appointed as personal guardian of my child(ren) _____ [child(ren)'s name]. If _____ [personal guardian's name] cannot serve as guardian, I nominate _____ [successor personal guardian's name] to be appointed as personal guardian for these children.
I nominate _____ [personal guardian's name] to be appointed as personal guardian of my child(ren) _____ [child(ren)'s name]. If _____ [personal guardian's name] cannot serve as guardian, I nominate _____ [successor personal guardian's name] to be appointed as personal guardian for these children.
I direct that no bond be required of any personal guardian.
I believe these people are the best personal guardians for the respective children because _____ [reasons].

_____ . *Gifts to Minors Under the Uniform Transfers to Minors Act.* All property left in this will to _____ [minor's name] shall be given to _____ [custodian's name] as custodian for _____ [minor's name] under the Uniform Transfers to Minors Act of _____ [your state]. If _____ [custodian's name] cannot serve as custodian, _____ [successor custodian's name] shall serve as custodian.

* Addition: Varying the Age at Which Minor Receives Gift

The custodianship for _____ [minor's name] shall end when _____ [she/he] becomes age _____ [specify age allowed by your state].

_____ . *Family Trust.* All property I leave by this will to the children listed in Section A below shall be held for them in a single trust, the family trust.

A. Trust Beneficiaries

_____ [child's name]

_____ [child's name]

_____ [child's name]

(continued on next page)

(PERSONAL WILL CLAUSES continued from previous page)

If all of the beneficiaries of the family trust are age 18 or older at my death, no family trust shall be established, and the property left to them shall be distributed to them outright.

If a beneficiary survives me but dies before the family trust terminates, that beneficiary's interest in the trust shall pass to the surviving beneficiaries of the family trust.

B. **Trustee of the Family Trust.** The trustee shall be _____ [trustee's name] or, if _____ [she/he] cannot serve as trustee, the trustee shall be _____ [successor trustee's name]. No bond shall be required of any trustee.

C. **Duties of the Family Trust Trustee**
   1. The trustee may distribute trust assets (income or principal) as the trustee deems necessary for a beneficiary's health, support, maintenance, and education. Education includes, but is not limited to, college, graduate, postgraduate, and vocational studies and reasonably related living expenses.
   2. In deciding whether or not to make distribution, the trustee shall consider the value of the trust assets, the relative current and future needs of each beneficiary and each beneficiary's other income, resources, and sources of support. In doing so, the trustee has the discretion to make distributions that benefit some beneficiaries more than others or that completely exclude others.
   3. Any trust income that is not distributed by the trustee shall be accumulated and added to the principal.

D. **Termination of the Family Trust.** When the youngest surviving beneficiary of this family trust reaches 18, the trustee shall distribute the remaining trust assets to the surviving beneficiaries in equal shares.

E. **Powers of the Trustee.** In addition to all other powers granted a trustee in any portion of this will, the trustee of the family trust shall have the power to make distributions to the beneficiaries directly or to other people or organizations on behalf of the beneficiaries.

_____ . *Child's Trust.* All Property I leave by this will to a child listed in Section A below shall be held for that child in a separate trust.

A. **Trust Beneficiaries and Age Limits.** Each trust shall end when the beneficiary becomes 35, except as otherwise specified.
   Trust for _____ [name] shall end at age _____ [age].
   Trust for _____ [name] shall end at age _____ [age].
(repeat as needed)

B. **Trustees.** The trustee for _____ [name of child or children] shall be _____ [trustee's name], or, if _____ [she/he] cannot serve as trustee, the trustee shall be _____ [successor trustee's name].
(repeat as needed)
No bond shall be required of any trustee.

C. **Duties of the Trustee**
   1. The trustee may distribute trust assets (income or principal) as the trustee deems necessary for the beneficiary's health, support, maintenance, and education. Education includes, but is not limited to, college, graduate, postgraduate, and vocational studies, and reasonable related living expenses.
   2. In deciding whether or not to make a distribution, the trustee may take into account the beneficiary's other income, resources, and sources of support.
   3. Any trust income that is not distributed by the trustee shall be accumulated and added to the principal of that child's trust.

(PERSONAL WILL CLAUSES continued from previous page)

D. **Termination of Trust.** A child's trust shall terminate when any of the following events occur:
1. the beneficiary becomes the age specified in Section A of this trust clause;
2. the beneficiary dies before becoming the age specified in Section A of this trust clause; or
3. the trust is exhausted through distributions allowed under these provisions.

If the trust terminates for reason one, the remaining principal and accumulated net income of the trust shall pass to the beneficiary. If the trust terminates for reason two, the remaining principal and accumulated net income of the trust shall pass to the trust beneficiary's heirs.

E. **Powers of the Trustee.** In addition to all other powers granted the trustee in this will, the trustee shall have the power to make distributions to a child's trust beneficiary directly or to other people or organizations on behalf of that child.

_____ . *General Trust Administrative Provisions.* Any trust established under this will shall be managed subject to the following provisions.

A. **Intent.** It is my intent that any trust established under this will be administered independently of court supervision to the maximum extent possible under the laws of the state having jurisdiction over the trust.

B. **No Assignment.** The interests of any beneficiary of any trust established under this will shall not be transferable by voluntary or involuntary assignment by operation of law and shall be free from the claims of creditors and from attachment, execution, bankruptcy, or other legal process to the fullest extent permitted by law.

C. **Trustee's Powers.** In addition to all other powers granted the trustee in this will, the trustee shall have all the powers generally conferred on trustees by the laws of the state having jurisdiction over this trust and the powers to:
1. Invest and reinvest trust funds in every kind of property and every kind of investment, provided that the trustee acts with the care, skill, prudence, and diligence under the prevailing circumstances that a prudent person acting in a similar capacity and familiar with such matters would use.
2. Receive additional property from any source and acquire or hold properties jointly or in undivided interests or in partnership or joint venture with other people or entities.
3. Enter, continue, or participate in the operation of any business, and incorporate, liquidate, reorganize, or otherwise change the form or terminate the operation of the business and contribute capital or loan money to the business.
4. Exercise all the rights, powers, and privileges of an owner of any securities held in the trust.
5. Borrow funds, guarantee, or indemnify in the name of the trust and secure any obligation, mortgage, pledge, or other security interest, and renew, extend, or modify any such obligations.
6. Lease trust property for terms within or beyond the term of the trust.
7. Prosecute, defend, contest, or otherwise litigate legal actions or other proceedings for the protection or benefit of the trust; pay, compromise, release, adjust, or submit to arbitration any debt, claim, or controversy; and insure the trust against any risk and the trustee against liability with respect to other people.
8. Pay himself or herself reasonable compensation out of trust assets for ordinary and extraordinary services, and for all services in connection with the complete or partial termination of this trust.
9. Employ and discharge professionals to aid or assist in managing the trust and compensate them from the trust assets.

(continued on next page)

(PERSONAL WILL CLAUSES continued from previous page)

D. **Severability.** The invalidity of any provision of this trust instrument shall not affect the validity of the remaining provisions.

E. **"Trustee" Defined.** The term "trustee" includes all successor trustees.

Property Guardian

* **Alternative 1. One Property Guardian for All Children**

_____ . *Property Guardian.* If at my death any of my children are minors, and a property guardian is needed, I appoint _____ [property guardian's name] as property guardian of my minor children. If _____ [she/he] cannot serve as property guardian, I appoint _____ [successor property guardian's name] as property guardian.
I direct that no bond be required of any property guardian.

* **Alternative 2. Different Property Guardians for Different Children**

_____ . *Property Guardian.* If at my death any of my children are minors, and a property guardian is needed:
I appoint _____ [property guardian's name] as property guardian of my minor child(ren) _____ [child(ren)'s name]. If _____ [property guardian's name] cannot serve as guardian, I nominate _____ [successor property guardian's name] to be appointed as property guardian for these children.
(repeat as needed)
I direct that no bond be required of any property guardian.

* **Addition: Explaining the Reasons for Your Choice**

I believe these are the best property guardians for these children because: _____ [reasons].

_____ . *No-Contest Clause.* If any beneficiary under this will in any legal manner contests or attacks this will or any of its provisions, any property, share, or interest in my estate left to the contesting beneficiary under this will is revoked and shall be disposed of as if that contesting beneficiary had predeceased me without children.

_____ *Simultaneous Death.* If my _____ [wife/husband/mate], _____ [name], and I should die simultaneously, or under such circumstances as to render it difficult or impossible to determine by clear and convincing evidence who predeceased the other, I shall be conclusively presumed to have survived my _____ [wife/husband/mate] for purposes of this will.

_____ . *Pets.* I leave my pet(s) _____ [pet's name(s)] to _____ [name or names].

* **Addition: Money for Your Pet's New Owner**

To help _____ [name or names] care for my pet(s), I also leave the sum of $_____ [amount] to _____ [him/her/them]. Other personal instructions: _____ .

SELF-PROVING AFFIDAVIT

STATE OF _____
COUNTY OF _____

I, the undersigned, an officer authorized to administer oaths, certify that _____ , the testa-tor, and _____ , _____ , and _____ , the witnesses, whose names are signed to the attached or foregoing instrument and whose signatures appear below, having appeared to-gether before me and having been first duly sworn, each then declared to me that: 1) the at-tached or foregoing instrument is the last will of the testator; 2) the testator willingly and voluntarily declared, signed, and executed the will in the presence of the witnesses; 3) the wit-nesses signed the will upon request by the testator, in the presence and hearing of the testator, and in the presence of each other; 4) to the best knowledge of each witness the testator was, at that time of the signing, of the age of majority (or otherwise legally competent to make a will), of sound mind and memory, and under no constraint or undue influence; and 5) each witness was and is competent and of the proper age to witness a will.

Testator: _____

Witness: _____
Address: _____
              _____

Witness: _____
Address: _____
              _____

Witness: _____
Address: _____
              _____

Subscribed, sworn, and acknowledged before me by _____ , the testator, and by _____ ,
_____ , and _____ , the witnesses, this _____ day of _____ , 20_____ .

Signed: _____
_____ [official capacity of officer]

FIRST CODICIL TO THE WILL
OF _____

I, _____ [your name], a resident of _____ [city], _____ [state] declare this to be the first codicil to my will dated _____ [date of will].

FIRST: I revoke the provision of Clause _____ of my will that provided:
_____ [Include the exact language you wish to revoke]

SECOND: I add the following provision to Clause _____ of my will:
_____ [Add whatever is desired]

THIRD: In all other respects I confirm and republish my will dated _____ [month/day], _____ [year].

I subscribe my name to this codicil this _____ [day] day of _____ [month], _____ [year] at _____ [city], _____ [county], _____ [state] and do hereby declare that I sign and execute this codicil willingly, that I execute it as my free and voluntary act for the purposes therein expressed, and that I am of the age of majority or otherwise legally empowered to make a codicil and under no constraint or undue influence.

Signature

_____ [your signature]

Witnesses

On this _____ [day] day of _____ [month], _____ [year], _____ [your name] declared to us, the undersigned, that this instrument was the codicil to _____ [his/her] will and requested us to act as witnesses to it. _____ [He/She] thereupon signed this codicil in our presence, all of us being present at the same time. We now, at _____ [his/her] request, in _____ [his/her] presence and in the presence of each other, subscribe our names as witnesses and declare we understand this to be _____ [his/her] codicil and that to the best of our knowledge _____ [he/she] is of the age of majority, or is otherwise legally empowered to make a codicil and is under no constraint or undue influence.
We declare under penalty of perjury that the foregoing is true and correct. This _____ [day] day of _____ [month], _____ [year], at _____ [city], _____ [state].

_____ [witness's signature]

_____ [witness's typed name] residing at _____ [street address], _____ [city], _____ [county], _____ [state].

_____ [witness's signature]

_____ [witness's typed name] residing at _____ [street address], _____ [city], _____ [county], _____ [state].

_____ [witness's signature]

_____ [witness's typed name] residing at _____ [street address], _____ [city], _____ [county], _____ [state].

DURABLE POWER OF ATTORNEY FOR FINANCES

KNOW ALL MEN BY THESE PRESENTS:

That I, _____ , the undersigned principal, whose address is _____ , by this instrument, hereby constitute and appoint, _____ , whose address is _____ , as my agent to act in my name, place, and stead, and for my use and benefit as if I were personally present to accomplish the same.

I specifically authorize, although not limited thereby, my above named agent to:

A. ask, collect, demand, receive, recover, and sue for all such sums of money, debts, accounts, legacies, bequests, interest, dividends, annuities, and demands whatsoever as are now, or shall hereafter become due, owing, payable, or belonging to me; to have, use, and take all lawful ways or means necessary to grant acquittance or other sufficient discharges for the same;

B. bargain, contract, purchase, receive, sell, possess, convey, transfer, lease, let, demise, remise, assign, release, encumber, hypothecate, mortgage, or otherwise exercise any property right in any and all types, kinds, and descriptions of both real and personal property, in lands, tenements, hereditaments, attachments, equipment, goods, wares, choses in action, personality, or other property in possession or in action;

C. sign, seal, deliver, or otherwise execute and/or acknowledge any agreement, bottomry, bill, bill of lading, bond, charter, contract, covenant, deed, debt instrument, demand, indenture, judgment, note, notice, pledge, protest, receipts, release, satisfaction of mortgage, or any other such instruments in writing as may be necessary or proper to fully accomplish these premises;

D. deposit, withdraw, pledge, or otherwise collect, recover, or hypothecate any and all monies held in my name in any bank, savings and loan association, trust company, thrift institution, loan company, brokerage firm, insurance company, or any other financial institution or an individual or firm acting in a fiduciary capacity in regards to any such monies now due, owing, payable, or otherwise belonging to me;

E. exercise any rights, options, or privileges available to me under or in connection with any annuity, contract, disability award, accumulated retirement contract, or life insurance policy, including, but not limited to, the right to amend, change, or modify the manner, method, or frequency of payments under such contract, and to surrender, pledge, or change the beneficiary under any such life insurance policy or policies;

F. invest and reinvest my money in any debt or equity security, such as stocks, bonds, debentures, treasury bills, treasury notes, trust certificates, certificates of deposit, joint ventures, mortgages, deeds of trust, limited partnerships, or contract services.

GIVING AND GRANTING unto said Agent, full power and authority to transact any business, perform every act and thing whatsoever requisite and necessary to fully accomplish the intents and purposes of this Power of Attorney, and therefore, I hereby ratify and confirm every act that said Agent shall lawfully do or cause to be done by virtue of these presents.

The validity of this Power of Attorney shall not be affected by my subsequent disability or incapacity or the lapse of time, and shall continue in full force and effect during my lifetime, unless sooner revoked or terminated by me in writing.

IN WITNESS WHEREOF, I, have hereunto set my hand this _____ day of _____ , 20 _____ .

_____	_____
Signature of Witness	Signature of Principal
_____	_____
Address of Witness	Address of Principal
_____	_____
City/State/Zip Code	City/State/Zip Code

(continued on next page)

(DURABLE POWER OF ATTORNEY FOR FINANCES continued from previous page)

ACKNOWLEDGMENT OF PRINCIPAL

I, _____ , the principal, sign my name to this power of attorney this

_____ day of _____ , 20_____ , and being first dully sworn, do declare to the undersigned authority that I sign and execute this instrument as my power of attorney and that I
sign it willingly, or willingly direct another to sign for me, that I execute it as my free and voluntary act for the purposes expressed in the power of attorney and that I am eighteen years of
age or older, of sound mind, and under no constraint or undue influence.

_____
Signature of Principal

AFFIDAVIT OF WITNESS

I, _____ , the witness, sign my name to the foregoing power of attorney

being first duly sworn and do declare to the undersigned authority that the principal signs and
executes this instrument as his/her power of attorney and that he/she signs it willingly, or willingly directs another to sign for him/her, and that I in the presence and hearing of the principal, sign this power of attorney as witness to the principal's signing and that to the best of my
knowledge the principal is eighteen years of age or older, of sound mind, and under no constraint or undue influence.

_____
Signature of Witness

State of _____)
)ss.
County of _____)

SUBSCRIBED, SWORN TO, AND ACKNOWLEDGED before me by _____ , the principal,
and subscribed and sworn to before me by _____ , the witness, this _____ day of
_____ , 20 _____ .

My Commission Expires: _____

_____
Notary Public

NEW YORK LIVING WILL

TO: MY FAMILY, MY PHYSICIAN, MY ATTORNEY, MY AGENT, AND ALL OTHERS WHOM IT MAY CONCERN:

(1) Print Your Name

I, _____ , being of sound mind make this statement as a directive to be legally binding if I can no longer make and/or communicate informed decisions regarding my medical care. These instructions express my strong and durable commitment to refuse medical treatment and to accept the consequences of such refusal under the circumstances indicated below.

(2) Cross Out Any Statements with Which You Do Not Agree

A. I instruct my attending physician to withhold or withdraw treatment that merely prolongs my dying:

  1. If I should be in an incurable or irreversible mental or physical condition with no reasonable expectation of recovery; AND
  2. If I am:

   a. In a terminal condition;
   b. Permanently unconcious;
   c. In a condition where life-sustaining procedures would be medically futile; or
   d. Minimally conscious but have enough irreversible brain damage such that I will never regain the ability to make and/or communicate my decisions and my wishes.

B. Furthermore, I direct that:

   a. I be allowed to die from the underlying conditions or illnesses and to not have my death prolonged through medical intervention;
   b. I be given maximum pain relief to keep me comfortable and to alleviate pain and suffering, even if this may shorten my remaining life;
   c. I receive maximum pain medication for any pain or discomfort stemming from the withholding of withdrawing of medical procedures including artificial nutrition and hydration;
   d. If I should execute a Health Care Proxy, such document shall be construed together with this Living Will; and
   e. If there is any doubt as to whether or not life-sustaining treatment is to be administered to me, it be resolved in favor of withholding or withdrawing such treatment.

C. While I understand that I am not legally required to be specific about future treatment and that I cannot foresee all possible examples of procedures, treatments, and medication, I feel especially strongly about and do not want, the following form(s) of treatment:

   a. cardiopulmonary resuscitation (CPR)
   b. artificial nutrition and hydration (tube feeding)
   c. mechanical respiration
   d. antibiotics

(3) Add Personal Instructions (if any)

_____

_____

(Unless your agent knows your wishes concerning artificial nutrition and hydration [tube feeding], your agent will *not* be allowed to make decisions about artificial nutrition and hydration. See booklet for samples of language you could use.)

(continued on next page)

(NEW YORK LIVING WILL continued from previous page)

(4) Sign and Date the Living Will and Print Your Address

These directions are the final expression of my legal right to refuse medical treatment and to accept the consequences of such refusal under the law of New York State. I intend my instructions to be carried out, unless I have withdrawn them in writing or by clear indication that I have changed my mind. This directive is in accordance with my strong convictions and beliefs and is made freely without any inducement or coercion from any person or institution.

Signature: _____

Address: _____

_____

Date: _____

WITNESSING PROCEDURE (MUST BE 18 OR OLDER) STATEMENT BY WITNESSES

(5) Sign and Date the Living Will and Print Your Address

I declare that I am eighteen years of age or older. The person who signed this document is personally known to me and he or she signed (or asked another to sign for him or her) this document in my presence. He or she appeared to be of sound mind and under no duress, fraud, or undue influence and appeared to sign the document willingly and with understanding of its contents.

Witness 1: _____

Address: _____

_____

Date: _____

Witness 2: _____

Address: _____

_____

Date: _____

LIVING WILL
AFFIDAVIT OF WITNESSES

The two witnesses, _____ and _____ , personally appeared before me and declared that they witnessed the execution of the Living Will of _____ on _____ and that he/she signed said Living Will, or asked another to sign said Living Will willingly and with understanding of its contents, while of sound mind and in all respects competent to make such Living Will and not under any duress, undue influence, or fraud.

The witnesses further state that at the time of the execution of this Affidavit, the witnesses identified the above-described Living Will by their signatures appearing thereon as subscribing witnesses.

Witness 1: _____

Address: _____

_____

_____

Date: _____

Witness 2: _____

Address: _____

_____

_____

Date: _____

Sworn to before me this

day of _____ , 20 _____

_____

Notary Public, State of New York

County of _____

NEW YORK HEALTH CARE PROXY

TO: MY FAMILY, MY PHYSICIAN, MY ATTORNEY, MY AGENT, AND ALL OTHERS WHOM IT MAY CONCERN:

(1) Print Your Name
    Print Name, Home Address and
    Telephone Number of Proxy Agent

I, _____ , hereby appoint:
                    (name)

_____

_____

_____
(name, home address, and telephone number of proxy)

as my health care agent to make any and all health care decisions for me, except to the extent that I state otherwise.

This proxy shall take effect in the event I become unable to make my own health care decisions.

(2) Add Personal Instructions (If Any)

I direct my proxy to make health care decisions in accordance with my wishes and limitations as stated below, or as he or she otherwise knows.

_____

_____

_____

_____

_____

(Unless your agent knows your wishes about artificial nutrition and hydration [tube feeding], your agent will *not* be allowed to make decisions about artificial nutrition and hydration. See booklet for samples of language you could use.)

(3) Print Name, Home Address, and Telephone Number of Your Alternate Proxy

Name of substitute proxy if the person I appoint above is unable, unwilling, or unavailable to act as my health care agent.

_____

_____

_____

_____
(name, home address, and telephone number of alternate proxy)

(4) Duration or Condition (if Any)

Unless I revoke it, this proxy shall remain in effect indefinitely, or until the date or conditions stated below. This proxy shall expire (specific date or conditions, if desired):

_____

_____

_____

_____

(NEW YORK HEALTH CARE PROXY continued from previous page)

(5) Sign and Date the Proxy and Print Your Address

Signature: _____

Address: _____

_____

_____

Date: _____

WITNESSING PROCEDURE STATEMENT BY WITNESSES (MUST BE 18 OR OLDER)

(6) Sign and Date the Health Care Proxy and Print Your Address

I declare that I am eighteen years of age or older. The person who signed this document is personally known to me and he or she signed (or asked another to sign for him or her) this document in my presence. He or she appeared to be of sound mind and under no duress, fraud, or undue influence and appeared to sign the document willingly and with understanding of its contents. I am not the person appointed as agent by this document.

Witness 1: _____

Address: _____

_____

_____

Date: _____

Witness 2: _____

Address: _____

_____

_____

Date: _____

HEALTH CARE PROXY
AFFIDAVIT OF WITNESSES

The two witnesses, _____ and _____ , personally appeared before me and declared that they witnessed the execution of the Health Care Proxy of _____ on _____ and that he/she signed said Health Care Proxy, or asked another to sign said Health Care Proxy willingly and with understanding of its contents, while of sound mind and in all respects competent to make such Health Care Proxy and not under any duress, undue influence, or fraud.

The witnesses further state that at the time of the execution of this Affidavit, the witnesses identified the above-described Health Care Proxy by their signatures appearing thereon as subscribing witnesses.

Witness 1: _____
Address: _____
_____
_____

Date: _____

Witness 2: _____
Address: _____
_____
_____

Date: _____

Sworn to before me this
day of _____ , 20 _____
_____

Notary Public, State of New York
    County of _____

STATE OF NEW YORK DEPARTMENT OF HEALTH
NONHOSPITAL ORDER NOT TO RESUSCITATE (DNR ORDER)

Person's Name _____

Date of Birth ____ / ____ / ____

Do not resuscitate the person named above.

Physician's Signature _____
Print Name _____
License Number _____
Date ____ / ____ / ____

It is the responsibility of the physician to determine, at least every 90 days, whether this order continues to be appropriate, and to indicate this by a note in the person's medical chart. The issuance of a new form is NOT required, and under the law this order should be considered valid unless it is known that it has been revoked. This order remains valid and must be followed, even if it has not been reviewed within the 90-day period.

DECLARATION AND INSTRUMENT OF A LIVING TRUST
FOR ONE PERSON

I. **Trust Name:** This trust shall be known as The _____ Trust.

II. **Trust Property:**

A. _____ , hereinafter called TRUSTEE, declares that he/she has set aside and holds in The _____ Trust all his/her interest in that property described in the attached Schedule A.

The trust property shall be used for the benefit of the trust beneficiaries, and shall be administered and distributed by the TRUSTEE in accordance with this trust instrument.

B. Additional property or property acquired after this Living Trust is declared may be added to the trust by listing it on the appropriate schedule.

III. **Reserved Powers of TRUSTEE:**

A. The Trustee reserves the power to amend or revoke this trust at any time during his/her lifetime, without notifying any beneficiary.

B. Until death of the TRUSTEE, all rights to income, profits, or control of the trust property shall be retained by or distributed to the TRUSTEE.

C. If at any time, as certified in writing by a licensed physician, the TRUSTEE has become physically or mentally incapacitated, the Successor Trustee shall manage this trust, and shall apply for the benefit of the TRUSTEE any amount of trust income, or trust principal, necessary in the Successor Trustee's discretion for the proper health care, support, maintenance, comfort, or welfare of the TRUSTEE, in accordance with his/her accustomed manner of living, until the TRUSTEE, as certified by a licensed physician, is again able to manage his/her own affairs, or until his/her death.

Any income in excess of amounts applied for the benefit of the TRUSTEE shall be accumulated and added to the trust property.

D. After the death of the TRUSTEE, this trust becomes irrevocable and may not be altered or amended in any respect unless specifically authorized by this instrument, and may not be terminated except through distributions permitted by this instrument.

IV. **Trustees:**

A. The TRUSTEE of The _____ Trust and all subtrusts created pursuant to Paragraph VI of this trust shall be _____ . Upon the death of the TRUSTEE or his/her incapacity as certified by a licensed physician, the Successor Trustee shall be _____ , or if he/she is unable to serve, or continue serving, as Successor Trustee, the Successor Trustee shall be _____ .

B. Any TRUSTEE shall have the right to appoint, in writing that shall be notarized, additional Successor Trustees to serve in the order nominated if all Successor Trustees named in Paragraph IV(A) cannot serve as TRUSTEE.

Declaration and Instrument of The _____ Trust

C. As used in this instrument, the term "TRUSTEE" shall include any Successor Trustee.

D. No bond shall be required of any TRUSTEE.

E. Except as provided in Paragraph VI(D)(2), no TRUSTEE shall receive any compensation.

V. Beneficiaries:

A. Upon the death of the TRUSTEE, the specific beneficiaries of The _____ Trust shall be:

1. _____ shall be given _____
_____

or, if said beneficiary doesn't survive the TRUSTEE, that property shall be given to _____ as alternate beneficiary.

2. _____ shall be given _____
_____

or, if said beneficiary doesn't survive the TRUSTEE, that property shall be given to _____ as alternate beneficiary.

3. _____ shall be given _____
_____

or, if said beneficiary doesn't survive the TRUSTEE, that property shall be given to _____ as alternate beneficiary.

4. _____ shall be given _____
_____

or, if said beneficiary doesn't survive the TRUSTEE, that property shall be given to _____ as alternate beneficiary.

5. _____ shall be given _____
_____

or, if said beneficiary doesn't survive the TRUSTEE, that property shall be given to _____ as alternate beneficiary.

6. _____ shall be given _____
_____

or, if said beneficiary doesn't survive the TRUSTEE, that property shall be given to _____ as alternate beneficiary.

B. The residuary beneficiary of the trust shall be _____ , who shall be given all trust property not specifically and validly disposed of by Paragraph V(A), or if said residuary beneficiary doesn't survive the TRUSTEE, the alternate residuary beneficiary shall be _____ .

C. Upon the death of the TRUSTEE, the Successor Trustee shall distribute the trust property outright to the beneficiaries named in Paragraphs V(A) and V(B), unless a beneficiary is a minor at the time of distribution, in which case that beneficiary's property shall be retained in trust according to the terms of Paragraph VI.

Declaration and Instrument of The _____ Trust

VI. Children's Trust Beneficiaries:

All trust property given in Paragraph V of this trust to any of the beneficiaries listed below in Section A shall be retained in trust for each such beneficiary in a separate subtrust of this _____ Trust. The following terms shall apply to each subtrust:

(continued on next page)

A. Subtrust Beneficiaries and Age Limits:

Each subtrust shall end when the beneficiary of that subtrust listed below becomes 35, except as otherwise specified in this section:

Subtrust for:	Ends at age:	Subtrust for:	Ends at age:
_____	_____	_____	_____
_____	_____	_____	_____
_____	_____	_____	_____
_____	_____	_____	_____

B. Distribution of Subtrust Funds:

1. Until a subtrust ends, the TRUSTEE may distribute from time to time to or for the benefit of the beneficiary as much, or all, of the net income or principal of the subtrust, or both, as the TRUSTEE deems necessary for the beneficiary's health, support, maintenance, or education.
   Education includes, but is not limited to, college, graduate, postgraduate, and vocational studies, and reasonably related living expenses.
2. In deciding whether to make a distribution to the beneficiary, the TRUSTEE may take into account the beneficiary's other income, resources, and sources of support.
3. Any subtrust income that is not distributed to a beneficiary by the TRUSTEE shall be accumulated and added to the principal of the subtrust administered for the beneficiary.

C. Termination of Subtrust: A subtrust shall terminate when any of the following events occur:

1. The beneficiary of that subtrust becomes the age specified in Paragraph VI(A).
2. The beneficiary of that subtrust dies before becoming the age specified in Paragraph VI(A).
3. The subtrust is exhausted through distribution allowed these provisions.

If the subtrust terminates for reason (1), remaining principal and accumulated net income of the subtrust shall be given outright to the beneficiary of that subtrust. If the subtrust terminates for reason (2), the remaining principal and accumulated net income of the subtrust shall pass to that subtrust beneficiary's heirs.

D. Subtrust Administrative Provisions:

1. The interests of subtrust beneficiaries shall not be transferable by voluntary or involuntary assignment or by operation of law and shall be free from the claims of creditors and from attachments, execution, bankruptcy, or other legal process to the fullest extent permitted by law.
2. Any TRUSTEE of a subtrust created under this Paragraph VI shall be entitled to reasonable compensation out of the subtrust assets for ordinary and extraordinary services, and for all services in connection with the termination of any subtrust.

VII. TRUSTEES Powers and Duties:

A. To carry out the provisions of The _____ Trust, and any subtrust created pursuant to Paragraph VI, the TRUSTEE shall have all authority and powers allowed or conferred on a TRUSTEE under the laws of the state of _____, and subject to the Successor Trustee's fiduciary duty to the TRUSTEE and the beneficiaries.
B. The TRUSTEE'S debts and death taxes shall be paid by the Successor Trustee from the following trust property:

(continued on next page)

(DECLARATION AND INSTRUMENT OF A LIVING TRUST FOR ONE PERSON continued from previous page)

If the property is insufficient to pay all the TRUSTEE'S debts and death taxes, the Successor Trustee shall determine how such debts and death taxes shall be paid.

VIII. General Administrative Provisions:

A. The validity of The _____ Trust and the construction of its beneficial provisions shall be governed by the laws of the State of _____ .

B. If any provision of this Trust is held to be unenforceable, the remaining provisions shall be nevertheless carried into effect.

Executed at _____ on _____ , A.D. _____
_____ TRUSTEE

I certify that I have read this Declaration and Instrument of Trust and that it correctly states the terms and conditions under which the trust estate is to be held, managed, and disposed of by the Successor Trustee. I approve the Declaration and Instrument of Trust.

Date: _____ , A.D. _____ .
_____ TRUSTEE

State of

                                    SS

County of

On, _____ before me, _____ ,
        [insert date]   [here insert name and title of office]

personally appeared _____ ,

❑ personally known to me, ❑ or proved to me on the basis of satisfactory evidence to be the person whose name is subscribed to the within instrument and acknowledged to me that he/she executed the same in his/her authorized capacity, and that by his/her signature on the instrument the person, or the entity upon behalf of which the person acted, executed the instrument.

WITNESS my hand and official seal.

Signature _____   [Seal]

SCHEDULE A

to

The Declaration and Instrument of

The _____ Trust

Glossary

abatement A priority system of reducing or eliminating bequests when an estate has insufficient funds to pay.

ademption Property left to a beneficiary in a will that is no longer in the decedent's estate at death.

administrator The person who is appointed by the probate court, when there is no will, to collect assets of the estate, pay its debts, and distribute the remainder to the beneficiary.

advance directives This is a general term that refers to any instruction or statement regarding future medical care.

affidavit A written statement of facts that is signed under oath before a notary public.

ancillary probate A probate proceeding conducted when the deceased person owns real estate in a state other than the one in which he resides.

appreciated property Property that has gone up in value since you bought it.

annual exclusion Under gift tax laws, each person may give as much as $10,000 per year to whomever he wishes.

augmented estate Property owned at the time of the person's death, as well as the value of any property transferred during his lifetime, not limited to the property passing by will.

beneficiary A person or organization selected to receive a portion of the estate under the terms of the will or trust.

bequest A gift of money or other property under the terms of a will or trust.

codicil An addition to a will, and like a will, it must be signed in front of witnesses.

community property In the states of Arizona, California, Idaho, Louisiana, Nevada, New Mexico, Texas, Washington, and Wisconsin, property that is acquired by husband and wife during their marriage, excluding gifts and inheritances. Each spouse has a one-half interest in their community property and therefore only one-half of such property can be disposed of by will.

community property with right of survivorship A special way for married couples to hold title to property, available in Arizona, Nevada, Texas, and Wisconsin. It allows one spouse's one-half interest in community property to pass to the surviving spouse without probate.

corporate trustee A professional organization, such as a bank or trust company, that receives, holds, and manages money and other property under a trust agreement.

creditor A person or organization to whom a deceased person owes money at the time of his death.

custodian A person authorized to manage assets given to or inherited by a child, under the Uniform Transfers to Minors Act.

decedent Someone who has died.

decree A court order.

disinheriting When the grantor (testator) cuts someone out of his will. A spouse cannot legally disinherit another spouse, but a parent can disinherit a child.

domicile The permanent resident of a person or the place to which he intends to return even though he may reside elsewhere.

estate The property you own when you die.

execution Making a written document complete by meeting the legal requirement of the completion. Usually achieved by signing, witnessing, and notarizing.

executor A person or organization named in a will to handle the settlement of the estate according to the will.

family trust A trust agreement that provides for a certain portion of the estate to be set aside in a separate trust to operate for the benefit of the family.

federal estate and gift tax A tax imposed by the federal government on people who give away or leave more than $675,000 to $1 million, depending on the year of death.

fiduciary Anyone responsible for the custody or management of property belonging to others, such as a trustee, executor, custodian, guardian of the person, and guardian of the property.

funding The transfer of property to a trust, without which the trust is not effective.

gift tax A tax imposed on transfers of property by gift during a person's lifetime.

grantor Someone who creates a trust. Also called testator or settlor.

gross estate The value of all property left by the deceased person required to be included in his estate for estate tax purposes.

health care proxy A legal document that allows a competent adult to appoint someone he trusts to make decisions about his medical care, including decisions about life-sustaining treatment, if he becomes unable to make these decisions for himself. The person you appoint is called the agent.

heir A person entitled by law to inherit under the will.

incompetent A person who is unable to handle his own affairs.

inter vivos trust A trust created while the grantor is still alive—a living trust.

intestate Someone who dies without making a valid will is said to die intestate. If a person dies intestate (without a will), the estate is distributed according to the laws governing intestate succession. Intestate succession is the method of distributing property to the closest surviving relatives, when a person fails to leave a valid will.

joint property Any property in joint ownership form.

legacy A clause in a will directing the disposition of money.

lien A legal claim against your property.

living trust A probate-avoiding device you create while you are alive and over which you have complete control. At your death, the property owned by the trust passes to your beneficiaries without going through probate.

living will Your personal statement about what medical treatment you want or do not want should you become incompetent and unable to make these decisions for yourself.

marital deduction A deduction allowed by federal estate law for all property passed to a surviving spouse. This deduction allows estate tax to be paid only after the death of the second spouse.

marital deduction trust A trust established to receive an amount on behalf of the surviving spouse that qualifies for the marital deduction.

minor In most states, a person under the age of 18.

net estate The value of all property owned at death minus liabilities.

no-contest clause A clause in a will or trust providing that any beneficiary who contests the document unsuccessfully will forfeit his share.

notary public Someone authorized by state law to witness signatures on legal documents and to sign them as evidence of the signature's validity.

personal property All property except real estate.

pour-over will A will used in conjunction with a revocable living trust to pour-over or transfer to the trust any assets that were not transferred to the trust before death.

power of attorney A document by which one person grants to another the legal right to act on his or her behalf with regard to specific situations. There is a power of attorney for financial decision making as well as one for medical decision making.

probate The procedure in each state required to settle legally the estate of a deceased person and transfer his probate property.

probate property All assets owned at death that require some form of court proceeding before title may be transferred to the beneficiaries.

real property Real estate

revocable trust A trust that can be revoked and amended at any time by its creator—a living trust.

rights of survivorship The rights of a joint tenant (but not a tenant in common) to take the whole of the jointly held property if he survives the other joint tenant(s).

securities Stocks and bonds.

tenancy by the entirety A type of joint ownership of property that can only be created between married individuals.

tenancy in common A type of joint ownership where two or more parties own the same property at the same time, not always in equal shares. There is no right of survivorship, so the deceased cotenant's share passes through his own estate.

testator (male) or testatrix (female) The name of a person who has created a legally valid will.

trust A legal entity in which one person (the trustee) is the holder of the legal title to property (the trust property) to keep or use for the benefit of another person (the beneficiary).

trustee An individual or organization that holds the legal title to the property in the trust for the benefit of another person(s).

undue influence Persuading a person to make changes in his will that he otherwise would not have made.

Uniform Transfers to Minors Act State laws adopted by many but not all states that allow you to appoint a custodian to hold property for the benefit of a minor.

will A document, signed and witnessed as required by law, that allows you to state who you want to inherit your property. Although this is its main purpose, it has other important uses as well. A will is a part of your probate property and as such must pass though the probate process when you die.

ABOUT THE AUTHOR

MARY CLEMENT is a New York attorney and co-author with Derek Humphry of *Freedom to Die: People, Politics and the Right-to-Die Movement,* published by St. Martin's Press in 1998. She is an expert on right-to-die issues and is an outspoken advocate of protecting self-determination and autonomy in matters of personal health. Ms. Clement has written amicus briefs for the United States Supreme Court, the Ninth and Second Circuit Courts of Appeals, and the Supreme Court in Alaska.

She is also President of Gentle Closure, Inc., an organization that helps people address end-of-life concerns, including living wills, health care proxies, nonhospital do-not-resuscitate orders, anatomical gifts, consultations for the removal of unwanted medical treatment, wills, and estate planning. Detailed question and answer booklets prepared by Ms. Clement accompany customized advance directive documents.

Ms. Clement is a member of the Board of Directors of the Hemlock Society and its sister organization, PRO USA. She is also on the Board of Directors of the Euthanasia Research & Guidance Organization (ERGO!). Ms. Clement has written articles for *The New York Times* and *The World Federation of Right-to-Die Societies Newsletter* and other publications, and has appeared on radio and television as an expert supporter of physician aid-in-dying for the terminally ill. Television appearances include *Court TV* and CNBC's *Equal Time*. She is a frequent lecturer on end-of-life issues at such places as the Association of the Bar of the City of New York.

Ms. Clement started law school twenty-four years after graduating from college, fulfilling a long-held dream. She was admitted to the New York Bar in 1993, the same month she turned fifty. She lived all her life in Manhattan until she moved to Sedona, Arizona, in 1996. She has two grown sons and one terrific Burmese cat, Picasso.

Gentle Closure, Inc.
60 Santa Susana Lane
Sedona, Arizona, 86336
Tel: (520) 282-0170
Fax: (520) 282-0286
Marydclem@aol.com

INDEX